FROGS WITHOUT LEGS CAN'T HEAR

NURTURING DISCIPLES IN HOME AND CONGREGATION

DAVID W. ANDERSON
AND
PAUL HILL

Augsburg Fortress
PUBLISHERS

FROGS WITHOUT LEGS CAN'T HEAR
Nurturing Disciples in Home and Congregation

Editors: Jeffrey S. Nelson, Ivy M. Palmer
Cover and text design: David Meyer

ISBN 0-8066-4649-7

Manufactured in the U.S.A.

11 10 09 08   7   8   9   10

We dedicate this book to our families
who have loved and put up with us
even as we have used them as living laboratories
for many of the ideas found in this book.

Our wives,
Gloria Anderson and Elaine Hill,
seem intuitively to know and live what we have written.
Thank you for being patient teachers.

Our children,
Kirsten Anderson-Stembridge and husband Matt Anderson-Stembridge,
Jeremy Anderson, and Josh and Amber Hill,
have kept us real and tolerated our experimentation well.
We feel blessed beyond measure for our families.

CONTENTS

FOREWORD

I still remember the day Carolyn and I were married. We were being married in a congregation that we did not know. Carolyn's family had moved to Phoenix, Arizona, after
her father was called to serve as pastor of Hope Church six months before our wedding.
We wondered, who would be there? We knew that there would be some family and
friends: parents, siblings, aunts, uncles, and a few friends from college. But there were
surprises! I remember looking at the church parking lot an hour before the wedding,
and there was a familiar Ford Thunderbird that looked like my Dad's father's car.
Grandpa Tom and *Crescent* (the t-bird) had driven over 1,000 miles to be there. While
greeting them, the pastor from my high school and college years arrived with family in
tow. To top it off, the church was filled with a welcoming community from my future
father-in-law's new parish!

Our wedding was an amazing mix of family, congregation, and community, which was
all gift. As you begin to read *Frogs Without Legs Can't Hear: Nurturing Disciples in
Home and Congregation,* I invite you to engage it as a gift that is being birthed, much
like our wedding day.

The denomination I represent, the Evangelical Lutheran Church in America, has roots
that go back to the settling of our nation, and beyond that to the reforming movement
of the sixteenth century in northern Europe. But at the same time, our church is just
moving into adolescence. Part of the reason for this adolescence is that the denomination is relatively young—just 15 years old at this writing. But the major reason for this
adolescence is that we live in the postmodern era in which we are trying to claim elements from the past that we value to assist the Spirit of God in establishing God's reign
for this new age. It is through family, congregation, and community that many of us
were brought to faith, but it seems that in the past 25 years disconnections have
occurred. We have given greater value to one source of faith over another, and have
missed crucial connections that bring full life in God.

I have read this book with thankfulness and surprise that the spirit of God is at work in children, youth, family, congregation, and community in ways more comprehensive than we can imagine. We have been given the great opportunity to be caught by the Spirit's power, reflected in this book; to be led to revitalized faith practices and principles that help pass on the faith given through God's grace.

As this book comes to you, our denomination has identified that ministry to and with children, youth, young adults, and family (in its widest sense) is central to passing on the faith from one generation to the next. I am grateful that this book can help us more effectively to integrate the wholeness that God desires for the creation into our lives and practices. I pray that God's Spirit will engage you through this new resource to assist you in more effectively passing on the faith in the places you live.

William Kees
Director, Youth and Gathering Team
Evangelical Lutheran Church in America

INTRODUCTION

As a way of introducing this book we begin with a contention: the church has been operating with a rather odd and ineffective understanding of who it is and how it operates in the world. The aspects of the church's self-image that we believe to be misguided reflect more about modern culture and institutional life than they do their biblical and historical roots. We also believe that the church's inaccurate perceptions about what it is as a faith community have led to numerous roadblocks for the evangelism and discipleship of the church. A vision of the church has existed for some time now that compromises and frustrates congregational and national church leaders, alienates the laity in the pews, and inhibits the Christian life in and around the homes of the faithful.

One objective of this book is to replace a historically recent and dominant vision of the church with one that better serves the well-being of the congregation and the home. The expectation is that through this alternative vision for the church we will—by the grace and work of God—as parents and pastors, congregational leaders, and the mentors of our children and youth, more effectively pass on faith, values, and character formation from generation to generation. Our confidence is based on over 10 years of using this vision as the basis for our work with congregational leaders, families, and youth. We see positive changes happening in homes and congregations. This confidence is only growing as congregations and households are themselves recognizing that the way we have been operating as congregations and as family units has not been adequate to the task of passing on the faith or raising our children.

As we often say to the communities with whom we work, the alternative vision and the changes we recommend are not rocket science, but a return to the basics. We believe this is the point of Matthew 13:52, where a scribe of the kingdom is described as one who brings out from his treasure what is old and what is new. Our goal is to bring together for our time what is well grounded in the Christian faith in a way that speaks to today's needs.

Through our work we have learned that the vision for the church described in this book has cross-generational, ecumenical, and international appeal. We use the phrase "cross-generational" rather than "inter-generational" with a specific double meaning intended. The secular world speaks of the value of inter-generational connections. We add a theological twist to the concept. Christian community is certainly inter-generational, but because it is a faith-formative community, it is marked by and linked to the cross of Christ. Throughout this book we will use the term "cross-generational" to lift up this distinctive character of inter-generational life in the church. Difference between "inter" and "cross"?

This cross-generational, ecumenical, and international vision endorses a style of communal living that can shape the life, health, and ministry of our congregations as well as the life, health, and ministry of our homes. The good news is that this vision is, in fact, already emerging in the lives of many individuals and congregations. This book simply offers language, principles, and strategies consistent with the emerging vision to help guide effective ministry for the twenty-first century in our homes and congregations.

THE FROG LEGS STORY

But first, we need to tell an amphibian tale and explain its significance for this book:
A mad scientist wanted to learn about the leaping abilities of frogs. To do so, he placed a frog on his laboratory table, stood behind the frog and shouted, "Jump, frog, jump!" The frog jumped. The scientist carefully measured the distance of that first leap. He consistently repeated this procedure a number of times to provide reliable and valid statistical research. He then surgically removed one of the front legs of the frog. (We know. It is a bizarre story. Remember, this is a *mad* scientist!) Placing the frog on the table, the scientist once again stood behind him and yelled, "Jump, frog, jump!" Again, responding to the noise, the frog leaped forward and the scientist carefully measured the distance.

The scientist had the frog jump with three legs a number of times to gather his scientific data. He then surgically removed another leg of the frog and repeated the experiment. He repeated each step of the experiment, measuring the ability of the frog to jump with four, then three, then two, then one leg. Finally, the scientist cut off the last leg and placed the frog on the table, stood behind the frog and yelled, "Jump, frog, jump!" Not surprisingly, the frog did not leap. The scientist yelled again but there was no response. The scientist finally stomped his feet, clapped his hands, and screamed as loudly as he could, but still the frog did not move. The scientist reflected on what he had seen and contemplated the meaning of this experiment. Finally, he sat up straight in his chair, and with an excited expression on his face that disclosed his discovery of new scientific insight, he wrote down, "Frogs without legs can't hear."

This story (probably older than the hills) was told by one of our nephews who had heard it in his high school biology class. The intent of this story was to emphasize that simply having data is not enough to draw sound scientific conclusions. The tale was a caution against running wild with partial information. Obviously the scientist in the story missed the point. He drew an erroneous conclusion because he had a poor image of what a frog is, assuming that a frog could jump without legs. This scientist apparently thought that it was enough to look like a frog to be able to jump like a frog; it was enough that the frog had a frog's head and a frog's torso. It was not necessary for the frog to have legs to be able to jump.

As outlandish as that idea might be, those of us in the church have made an equally silly conclusion. (We know that the right answer is: *frogs without legs lose their fear of loud noises and yelling.*) If we continue with the frog imagery and compare the body of the church with the body of a frog, we can perceive some similarly ridiculous conclusions. The church has assumed that if the church frog has a church frog head (church leadership) and a church frog torso (publicly gathered and visible community, primarily Sunday mornings in the congregation), that it should be able to jump and move in the world. The church seems to have missed the point that to be mobile in this world and, therefore, impact the larger world, the church frog needs church frog legs. The nature of those legs and how to exercise them is the point of this book.

The church is trying to leap into faithful congregational ministry for the twenty-first century without legs to propel it. Try as it might to move forward, too often the church just sits there. It seems to have lost the mobility of its legs. A body without any strength in the legs is immobile, and legs without a body have no purpose. The body and legs of the church need to come together to form a healthy, dynamic, and forward-leaping church. If the gospel of Jesus Christ is to be believed and passed on to the next genera-tions, then the whole church (or whole church frog) needs to be intact. The apostle Paul made a similar analogy and conclusion long ago (see 1 Corinthians 12:12-31). Today, a particular part of the church's body needs attention, support, and encouragement: the part of the church that lives day in and day out in the homes of the faithful.

Our conviction is that the church is made up of a partnership between the faith life in the home and the faith life of the congregation. The basic building block for healthy congregational life is the home, from where we routinely receive people into the public arena of the congregational setting. Christian faith and the life of faith are passed on from generation to generation through the symbiotic and coordinated efforts of the larger body working with the legs. This means that a closer relationship between home and congregation benefits both our homes and our congregations for healthier and more fulfilling faith in daily life. For our congregational leaders, this becomes foundational for evangelism and discipleship. For our parents, grandparents, mentors, and other caregivers of children, youth, and adults, this becomes the foundation for meaningful personal relationships that will impact the faith, values, and character formation of the faithful.

REASON FOR OPTIMISM

The image of the church frog implicitly conveys a very encouraging sign. The church is actually healthier than we often imagine. The church *has* legs, but often lacks ways to exercise them. The church tends to acknowledge the work of the church frog head (leadership development) and the church frog torso (public worship, Christian education programs, youth groups, and so on), but does not know how to exercise church frog legs. Similarly, attendance figures and budgets (both weak and inaccurate tools) are often used to measure church health and effectiveness. However, it is difficult to measure the faith life of Christians outside the sphere of congregational life. Perhaps measuring effectiveness—important as it is—has become an overvalued, modern penchant that needs to be qualified by the immeasurable work of the Holy Spirit.

Whether acknowledged and exercised or not, the church frog legs are there and they are moving, sometimes in spite of the head and the torso. Large numbers of adults want to make a difference with their lives and positively influence children and youth. Younger people are also on a quest to make a difference in this world, and faith is a part of their searching. Parents and children, grandparents and grandchildren, mentors and youth are trying—at times with great results. Their desire for meaning, hope, and faith in their daily life relationships can only be strengthened by a church that seeks to support and edify them in their vocation, their God-given calling, to bless the world with their lives of faith.

legs

IT'S ABOUT FAITH

In other words, it is all about faith. The primary evangelical task of the church is to pass on faith in Jesus Christ. The central question of the church is, "Are we forming faith?" Often the church skirts around this question. Pastors, youth ministers, teachers, and congregational guides are often asked instead, "Can you help us increase our church attendance?" or, "How can we get youth and families to come to church?" But these questions miss the mark. Only 20 percent of parents feel that congregations help families form faith![1] We cannot assume that what we are currently doing in our congregations is enough. Certainly church attendance and a vibrant corporate worship life are pieces of a healthy environment in which faith is formed. A healthy environment for faith formation is more complex than what takes place within the congregational walls, however. The faith life of the home is also critical. The term *home* for us is not merely the place where one lives and the people who live there. Rather, home is the larger network of relationships and daily life experiences of people of faith. Home is a metaphorical image to describe the intersection of faith and daily life. Parents are asking both implicitly and explicitly for their congregations to do more to help them create this healthy faith-formative environment.

The church tends to be preoccupied with what takes place within its institutional and physical walls, falsely assuming that within the congregational building, all the necessary elements are present and available for faith to be formed and flourish. Many church leaders and even everyday church members think in this way because this is the way they were raised to think. However, the Scriptures, church confessions, and church history, as well as recent research and anecdotal evidence, all show this to be a false assumption.

So, we are back to our question: "Are we forming faith?" The purpose of this book is to identify the principles and practices that are faith formative. We will present Five Principles, Four Key faith practices, and three characteristics of effective adult faith bearers to highlight the importance of faith in daily life, the faith lived in and out of our homes.

THE FIVE PRINCIPLES ARE:
1. Faith is formed by the power of the Holy Spirit through personal, trusted relationships, often in our own homes.
2. The church is a living partnership between the ministry of the congregation and the ministry of the home.
3. Where Christ is present in faith, the home is church, too.
4. Faith is caught more than it is taught.
5. If we want Christian children and youth, we need Christian adults and parents.

THE FOUR KEYS ARE:
1. Caring conversation
2. Devotions
3. Service
4. Rituals and traditions

THE THREE CHARACTERISTICS OF FAITH-BEARING ADULTS ARE:
1. Authenticity
2. Availability
3. Affirmation

Working through these Five Principles, Four Key faith practices, and three characteristics, the Holy Spirit creates passionate and faithful evangelists and disciples.

HOW TO READ THIS BOOK

In keeping with the guiding metaphor of the book, each chapter will be organized into sections called *Tadpole Tales, Lily Pad Roots,* and *Croaks, Ribbits, and Hops.*[2] By now you should be getting into the metaphor for the book.

Lily Pad Roots are the deep sections of the book. Just as lily pad roots anchor the plant securely in the pond, so these sections anchor our major themes in Scripture, research, and history. This is the deep content material.

Tadpole Tales are stories, anecdotes, and experiences we have had or heard which highlight, in a storytelling format, a specific point being made, usually in the *Lily Pad Roots* sections.

Croaks, Ribbits, and Hops are specific strategies and practices that make the principles come to life. They can be used as suggested, or may spark your own original ideas. Strategies for the principles and practices recommended in this book are seemingly infinite. We learn from those we teach, and we have seen some enormously creative ideas emerge.

With numerous challenges facing Christianity in our pluralistic society, it is necessary to reflect upon basic questions about how Christianity connects with people's lives in the twenty-first century. Such reflection is as basic as wondering how people gain a favorable impression of Christianity, feel welcomed into Christian fellowship, and, finally, go from being exposed to Christian faith to becoming Christians.

These are the fundamental questions that define and even divide various Christian communities today. However, this book seeks to explore this critical topic from such a basic biblical and experiential perspective that most Christians will be able to use the insights and recommendations within their own faith traditions. In fact, the contents of this book have been taught to Christian groups as diverse as Roman Catholics and Episcopalians to Mennonites, Baptist, and Pentecostals with very encouraging results. Living in a world that has become smaller through more convenient and affordable means of travel and instant communication, it is also encouraging that the information presented here has been well received by people from Africa, northern Europe, North America, and Australia.

We invite you to playfully and faithfully engage yourself along this creative journey.

NOTES

1. Gene Roehlkepartain, *Building Assets in Congregations* (Minneapolis: Search Institute, 1998), 125.
2. Chapters 1 and 2, which are foundational to the whole, do not include the section *Croaks, Ribbits, and Hops.*

CHAPTER ONE

Generic: A dynamic journey through which meaning is discovered.

Foundations:
So, what is faith?

Specific: The God-given vision of engaging the world through Jesus' eyes.

Tadpole Tale

Two friends, who had not seen each other for a long time, meet on the street. The one said to the other, "How have you been?" The other responds, "Fine, I've become a parent since the last time we were together." "That's great," says the friend. "Well, no," says the parent, "that's bad. I've never gone through such soul searching in my entire life." "Oh, that's bad," said the friend. "No, that's good," said the parent. "I've learned a lot about myself and my child." "Well, that's good," said the friend. "No, that's bad," said the parent. "I've not always liked what I've learned." "Oh, I know what you mean," said the friend. "That's bad." "Well, no, that's good," said the parent. "It reminds me that there is a merciful God out there, very tolerant of me." "Oh, well, that's good," said the friend. "Well, no, that's bad," said the parent. "I like being the center of my own universe." "Oh, yeah, I certainly understand that. That's bad," said the friend. "Well, no, that's good," said the parent. "When all is said and done, I need to know that the weight of the universe is not on my shoulders. I know I need a gracious God."

This dialogue articulates the immense highs and lows of parenting and faith.

What is faith? What are the characteristics of faith? Are there different types of faith? Is one kind better than another? Is having faith important? These are the deep and important questions that shape our lives as human beings and people of faith. Our assumption is that all human beings are people of some kind of faith. To be human is to be a person of faith. To be human is to be constantly in the "faithing" process. The pursuit of faith is as important to human life as eating and sleeping. Faith gives us our sense of hope and meaning for life; it is a way of seeing and interpreting and living in the world. It moves us, drives us, encourages us, comforts us, guides us, challenges us, and anchors us.

Sharon Daloz Parks, in her book *Big Questions, Worthy Dreams*, defines faith as "the dynamic composing of meaning."[1] Parks explains that human beings are creatures that must seek and find meaning. We are creatures that need to make sense of things. We perceive, evaluate, and organize our worlds in an ongoing search to understand who we are, where we are, why we are, and perhaps whose we are. Thus we are, by our very nature, faithful creatures. We cannot live without a sense of meaning. We are always on a journey that is dynamic, active, eventful, and fluid. The purpose of the journey is to "compose meaning," to figure out life. *Faith* is not so much a noun as it is a verb. We are always in the process of "faithing" or searching for meaning. So, faith isn't so much something we have than something we are always doing. Faith is the flow and energy of our lives in a never-ending process of integrating what we see, experience, learn, feel, sense, and wonder.

Parks adds that even as we journey, we also have need to belong. The human faithing process is rarely done alone, even in the highly individualistic American cultural context. The familiar story of the prodigal son (Luke 15:11-32) captures the idea of faith as a moving away from and a moving toward others. The younger brother strikes out on his own and journeys to a far away land, only to discover that his identity and future lies within the community from which he came. However, because of the journey he has taken, he reenters the community as a changed person. He is embraced and embraces the community of his past with new meaning, hope, commitments, and behavior. His is a faithing journey.

To be human is to be in the faithing process. James Ashbrook and Carol Albright, in referencing anthropologist Clifford Geertz, state, "It does appear that human beings are basically *homo religiosus*. We are symbolizing, conceptualizing, meaning-seeking animals."[2] This is human nature. Not surprisingly, religious surveys and polls consistently show that 90 percent of all Americans believe in God. This certainly makes sense if we are what God has made us—*homo religiosus*.

This insight is a great relief to parents and church leaders who are comforted to learn that God has hardwired the human creature to engage in faithing. What is distressing to parents and church leaders is to discover that increasingly, the faithing process is undertaken outside the structures and confines of organized religion and religious institutions. One woman told us: "I'm a very spiritual (read: faithing) person, but I don't have much time for organized religion." (One of us responded, "Would you prefer disorganized religion?" We did not win a convert.) To return to our metaphor, this woman was saying that the frog head and torso (leadership and gathered community) were not addressing her human need for faith. She needed legs for the journey.

Lily Pad Roots: Christian faith is more than a generic search for meaning

Humans are essentially religious and Christians claim that Jesus Christ is the focus of this human search. Christian faith gives particular definition, shape, and image to the generic human search for meaning. For Christians, faith is the God-given vision of engaging the world through Jesus' eyes. Faith is a gift, created by God and given freely (see Ephesians 2:8, "For by grace you have been saved through faith, and this is not your own doing; it is the gift of God . . ."). Second, faith is a way of looking at the world; a lens through which we view and interpret all that is around us. Faith brings into clearer focus the blurred and often confusing world in which we live. By the power of the Holy Spirit, our lives are opened to see through the cross of Christ beyond despair to hope; beyond condemnation to forgiveness; beyond senselessness to meaning; beyond hatred to reconciliation; beyond death to life. To see the world through Jesus' eyes does not mean we see clearly. Paul outlined the limits of faith vision, stating, "For now we see in a mirror, dimly . . ." (1 Corinthians 13:12). Rather, to see the world through Jesus' eyes is to have a glimpse of the will of God for God's people and all creation, which moves us to engagement to serve others, strive for justice, and work for peace.

Tadpole Tale: Camp counselors

This is the unique Christian claim and in our day it can create quite a scandal. We were working at a Lutheran camp one warm spring day, training 150 Lutheran young adults serving as camp staff for the coming summer. Our assignment with this group was to explain the core of Lutheran theology. We thought this to be a fairly easy assignment. At one point, we stated Luther's familiar theological theme that the place God chooses to reveal God's very self to the world is in the deep mystery of God, in Jesus Christ, suffering on the cross. No other place reveals the heart of God more deeply than here.

At this, the camp counselors became angry and animated, and for the next hour, we were fending for our lives as the unique claim of Christianity was questioned. "What about when I see God in a sunset?" one asked. "Is God not present in a drug abuse recovery program?" asked another. "God is most real to me in my meditation," protested a third. And on it went. Only after further reflection did we realize what we had run up against. All of these wonderful young adults were faithing, which we celebrate. But they were doing this faithing under a very common American assumption: all faith claims are true no matter the content; live and let live; don't dis (disrespect) me and I won't dis you. By making unique claims about Jesus, we were perceived as exclusionary rather than inclusive. Only after explaining that sunsets, recovery programs, and meditation were hidden and less direct ways in which Jesus nurtures our lives and world did the group relax—and then only somewhat.

Lily Pad Roots: Faith as trust, knowledge, and yielding

We want to be clear: this book is about faith formation centered in Jesus Christ. Parks gave a generic definition of faith as "the dynamic composing of meaning." We want to be more specific in our definition of faith: Faith is the God-given vision of engaging the world through Jesus' eyes.

The Protestant Reformation of the sixteenth century understood faith in this dynamic way through a three-part description—trust, knowledge, and yielding one's life. Faith incorporates specific information regarding the Triune God of the Bible and focuses on the central revelation of God in Jesus Christ, the Son of God. Faith also involves a way of life, a yielding to the work and will of God. The substance of such yielding is to praise God and serve God's created order with acts of love. In other words—and foundational to the reason for this book—faith is much more than subscribing to certain doctrines or expressing certain feelings and closeness to the God of the universe. And faith is more than good deeds. Faith is the lively, dynamic engagement of the whole person in the context of a whole faith community. This holistic understanding of faith as a way of life encourages and equips the faith journey in both the congregational and home contexts that we are addressing.

In other words, it takes a whole church frog to nurture this faithing process. A church frog without legs cannot carry the burden alone of passing the Christian faith to the next generation. It is not enough to have a church frog torso and a church frog head. The full-bodied church frog needs legs—the legs of the home, the legs of multiple generations, and the legs of Christian community—in order for faith to grow.

Lily Pad Roots: Styles of faith

Episcopal theologian John Westerhoff has identified four styles of faith.[3] Recognizing that faith takes different shapes, forms, and styles, Westerhoff affirms that faith is fluid, dynamic, and always emerging. This is the nature of being human; thus it is the nature of faith. The four styles are *experienced* faith, *affiliative* faith, *searching* faith, and *mature* faith.[4] Experienced faith, the first faith of children, is built around hugs, bonding, and experiences of trust. It grows out of our encounter and experience with other people, and is emotive and emotional. Though most closely identified with children, experienced faith is often seen in many adults as well.[5]

Affiliative faith is about identity rooted in an accepting community.[6] Within this community is a clear sense that one is wanted, important, and needed. Affiliative faith recognizes a strong authority, usually in the form of a pastor, the Bible, the church denomination, or the congregation. It emphasizes an experience of the heart, and is nurtured through story, song, music, and drama. Affiliative faith is the faith style of many church members. Those whose faith takes this form often describe church as a "family" or a place of sanctuary.

Searching faith is connected to adolescents and young adults. This faith style asks questions and is full of doubt.[7] Searching faith is the faith of experimentation. Often this faith looks with critical judgment upon any previous faith styles, content, or definitions. Searching faith is the faith style the church seems most to fear, but needs most to embrace if it wants to keep its young people. Those congregations that suppress questioning ultimately drive away the questioner. Retreats, interest groups, and service projects are effective means through which to engage those living this faith style.

Many adults as well as youth spend a lifetime in this style of faith. To some extent, this is necessary because one never leaves questions and doubts behind. Each new phase in life brings new experiences and issues that need to be addressed afresh by a vital and engaging faith. In fact, denying the necessity of a searching faith has greatly hindered faith life in the home. Many parents and other caregivers are simply not comfortable with their "little faith," so their own real questions remain hidden, the authenticity of their searching becomes shrouded, and the fundamental quality of being real and vulnerable is lost, thereby limiting genuine, loving, supportive, inquisitive relationships in the home. The truth of one's searching becomes a lie and little is left to share with one another on an intimate basis.

Mature faith is the result of cycling through the other three styles (imagine a corkscrew) and being so anchored in Christ that loving acts of service are routinely evident as fruits of the faith journey.[8] The hallmark of mature faith is the ability to do what one believes. According to Westerhoff, mature faith is rare and is seen in people like Mother Teresa, Dietrich Bonhoeffer, and Martin Luther King Jr., but others who have a mature faith that is often unrecognized also bless us. A colleague's story about his father's funeral serves to illustrate.

Tadpole Tale: Wisconsin bum

At the wake in a small Wisconsin town, the local "bum" made an unexpected and unwanted entrance. His name was Ernie. His face was dirty and unshaven, and he smelled bad. Certain family members asked that Ernie be escorted away from the wake. He was perceived as an obstruction to a precious and sacred moment. Instead, our colleague greeted Ernie and then watched him approach the casket. He touched the father's hand and said, "He was the most wonderful person I ever met." The family then heard the story of Ernie's relationship with their loved one. Every day for years, the father had gone to a local cafe for coffee at 10:00 A.M. Every day he left money with the cashier for a bowl of soup and sandwich for Ernie. On Wednesdays, he left Ernie a cigar in addition to the money for the meal. This story came as a total surprise to the family.

Our colleague was not surprised, however, by this revelation. In the weeks prior to his father's death he had been discovering dimensions of his father's faith and character that had never been disclosed to him before. For example, his father had requested that speakers be placed in his bedroom so he could listen to the hymns of the church as he lay in bed dying. When the son observed that his dad never sang the hymns in church, the father simply responded, "I never sang out loud." This man had a mature faith, though hidden from public view.

Westerhoff's styles of faith help us understand the nature of that which we wish to discuss in detail. The Five Principles and Four Keys are effective means to engage these styles of faith so that no matter the faith style, or how we move back and forth between these styles, the world is seen through the eyes of Jesus.

Lily Pad Roots: Parenting as a spiritual exercise

No matter where individuals and households are in their style(s) of faith, life is a faithing process that shapes us all one way or another. All of us experience life

as a spiritual journey. Parents and others who care for children on an intimate and regular basis especially exemplify this spiritual journey.

Those who care for children in their own homes never experience greater mountain-
tops and lower valleys than in the role of parent. Clearly these experiences are fraught
with spiritual material. It's important that parents not be isolated while going through
these intense relational and spiritual experiences. They need to know that God goes
with them and that the congregation will walk with them, help equip them, and prayer-
fully sustain them.

A fundamental outcome of this book is to take the weight of the universe off the shoulders of parents, grandparents, mentors, pastors, catechists—indeed, everyone who
cares about growing in grace and gracing the lives of children and youth with faith,
hope, and love. The church has too many souls walking around burdened like Jeremiah
anguishing over Jerusalem (see Lamentations 1). The church can and truly must lighten
the load of caring adults who want to nurture faith and values in homes and congregations. We expect the reader to walk away from this book saying, "I can do this. I can do
this in my home. I can do this in my congregation. I can do this in my relationship to
my world around me." Implicit in these *I* statements is a *we*: *we* can do this as a faith
community gathered in homes and congregations. We expect the reader to feel capable.
Understanding the Five Principles and doing the Four Keys are within one's grasp.

NOTES

1. Sharon Daloz Parks, *Big Questions, Worthy Dreams* (San Francisco: Jossey-Bass,
   2000), 137.
2. James Ashbrook and Carol Rausch Albright, *The Humanizing Brain* (Cleveland:
   Pilgrim Press, 1997), 35.
3. John Westerhoff, *Will Our Children Have Faith?* (Minneapolis: Winston Press,
   1976).
4. Ibid., 89.
5. Ibid., 91.
6. Ibid., 94.
7. Ibid., 96.
8. Ibid., 98.

CHAPTER TWO

Home and Congregation in Partnership: Introduction to the Five Principles

Lily Pad Roots: Going to church or being the church

The image of a church frog with legs is based on a different perception of church than the traditional understanding. Traditionally, church is a place to which one goes and in which certain leaders are present and activities are carried out. The problem with this limiting definition is that the people of God who are called to new life in Jesus Christ have a ministry, a message, and a way of life in and for the world that far exceeds what can take place "at church." But an understanding of church exists that is taught, preached, prayed, and sung differently than the way many local faith communities live out the idea of church. The former places emphasis on God's people being the church in daily life, including public gatherings of the faithful. The latter focuses on church as an institution identified through specific religious programs, policies, rituals, traditions, and gatherings that bring recognized leaders and members together for worship, education, service, or fellowship. The former is a process—random and chaotic; the latter is a sanctioned program—institutional and controlled. Both are legitimate expressions of the life of the church, but the church is limited in its ministry and outreach when it emphasizes only the institutional expression of the church to the exclusion of the church in daily life.

The consequence of the inconsistency between these two understandings of church is dramatic. Church leaders need to know that at times, vast differences exist between what the church wants to communicate in its teachings and what it actually teaches by the way it operates as a programmatic institution.

Tadpole Tale: Being with God

A group of second-graders and their parents were learning how to establish and maintain a life of prayer in the home. The class innocently began with a conversation starter to build relationships and trust between the adults and children. Two questions formed the conversation starter: "What is better about being an adult?" and "What is better about being a child?" One observant second grader responded, "What's better about being an adult is that adults get to be with God." Asked to elaborate, she said, "When we go to church, mom and dad go upstairs, and we go downstairs."

Clearly no one in her congregation—especially the clergy, other church professionals, and volunteer leaders—intended to teach her and other children that only adults get to be with God. But the way the congregation operated by splitting the membership between sanctuary and classroom sent a negative message. According to the observation of at least one second-grader, the message was clear: upstairs was the ornate and beautiful sanctuary with its marvelous music. To any reasonable second-grader, that space is understandably the "house of God." The sanctuary is, in fact, the location that most congregations invest their dollars, energies, and planning. "Invest" is a church word that has to do with how people "vest," that is, how they clothe themselves and their space. The vestments and the investments that take place in the sanctuary send a clear message: God is expected to be there.

By contrast, downstairs is where second-graders and many others attend Sunday school. The level of investment in that space is quite different. The basement classroom is a more austere setting (often including a moldy smell and paint-chipped walls), and is not as likely to be the dwelling place of God to the eyes of a second-grader. Adults get the prime cuts; children get the leftovers. The way the church operates may present a theology that is vastly inconsistent with the professed teaching of the church.

Lily Pad Roots: Sending mixed messages

The inconsistency in the message travels home with children. A popular children's song goes like this: "I am the church, you are the church, we are the church together. All who follow Jesus, all around the world, yes, we're the church together."* In Sunday school children may sing songs that suggest all are part of this church experience, but when they go home, the message again changes. The vernacular definition of the word *church* loses the larger community context and becomes reduced to a place

---

*Words: Richard Avery & Donald Marsh, © 1972 Hope Publishing Co, Carol Stream, IL 60188. All rights reserved. Used by permission.

and a time. The child hears, "Hurry up, or we'll (maybe you'll) be late for church." To experience the church, the child needs to get some other place at a certain time. This is quite different from "I am the church, you are the church, we are the church together."

To understand the church primarily as a people called to a way of life 24 hours a day, seven days a week emphasizes the union of home and congregation in a vital partnership in ministry and redefines the life and work of pastors, lay professionals, and lay volunteers in the congregation, as well as godparents, grandparents, parents, and other adult caregivers in the home, neighborhood, and community. All those who see themselves as part of this church benefit from a larger, more complete experience of church as the life of the people of God in various settings. This means a symbiotic relationship between the people publicly gathered in various congregational settings and the people interacting on a daily basis in the home and among different individuals, households, and communities. Church as presented here is a lively, interdependent partnership between the ministry of the congregation and the ministry of the home, the home being that generic term for families in all their diverse types and sizes and in their activity in daily life.

 Lily Pad Roots: Defining family and Christian parents

Please note that the word *family* is used in this book inclusively, not exclusively. The Bible uses a number of terms that are equated with our modern word for family. At the same time there is no Biblical word for the term family as we understand it today. The Hebrew and Greek terms are not restricted to a set of relationships bound by marriage, birth, or adoption in an immediate household environment. The Old Testament uses terms that equate family with extended domestic relationships, clan, tribe, and even the entire nation of Israel. The New Testament term for family may also be translated as "household" and would include extended family relationships as well as slaves and other workers in the economic life of the home.

We use the term "family" in this larger, more inclusive sense as a way to convey the immediate, personal, and trusted relationships that sustain people in life. As such, "family" includes not only two parents with children, but other configurations including single adults, single-parent families, multi-generational families, adoptive families, groups of friends, and various non-traditional configurations as well. Further, family includes the community of faith. In speaking of the early church understanding of family, the *Interpreter's Dictionary of the Bible* states,

> The importance of the family in biblical society and its function as the center of religious instruction account for the application of the term to Israel and to the community of Christ as the family of God. In the chapter that contains the essence of the so-called New Covenant the prophet writes of the time when Yahweh will be the God "of all the families of Israel, and they shall be [his] people" (Jeremiah 31:1). Early Christian writers continue the use of this figure by speaking of the Christians as comprising "God's family" (1 Timothy 3:15; 1 Peter 4:17).[1]

One consequence of this perspective of family is that every Christian adult is included under the category of Christian parent. All Christian adults are needed to support the parental activity of raising Christian children in the faith. A basic faith bond exists between Christian adults and children that fosters a filial relationship between them. Martin Luther considered this cross-generational bond between all Christian adults and children to be an essential requirement for faith formation and socialization. He stated, ". . . all who are called as masters stand in the place of parents and must derive from them their power and authority to govern."[2] "Masters" are Christian adults who join with parents in the vital work of raising children.

At the same time that we seek to be inclusive of and affirm the variety of forms and expressions of family life in today's culture, we also seek to uphold and strengthen the nuclear family composed of married couples and children. This basic unit of family relationships is an important element in the continuation of the human community and may still be considered a basic building block of the larger church. But in whatever form, families are the backbone of healthy society, and responsible family life is a powerful force.

Lily Pad Roots: Time of transition and evaluation

The church is the people of God who believe that Jesus is Lord and live out of this belief. As a unique, religious community in the world, the people of God have an opportunity to evaluate what it means to be and do the work of the church. The church frog with legs metaphor is a response to this need for reflection, assessment, and strategy. It is based on the premise that contemporary culture has entered into a post-Christian era in which the faith, language, symbols, rituals, and stories of Christianity can no longer be assumed to provide central core themes and values for society. No longer can one assume that people understand the basic biblical stories or teachings of the Christian faith. A new level of intentionality is required of the church in order to share the gospel of Jesus Christ with the world as well as with those within the household of faith.

This moment in time encourages the church to reflect further upon its biblical and historical roots and to assess the impact of contemporary experience on the life and work of the church. The vision in this book builds upon the biblical witness, Christian history and theology, and the insights of the behavioral sciences as well as personal experience to help energize both church leadership and the laity with a vision of the church rooted in the partnership between home and congregation.

This vision of church understands faith formation and mission to the larger world as an outgrowth of this partnership. It offers a foundational model for ministry that has been present since the beginning of the church and yet has been overlooked in our expert and professional-dependent modern world. This vision of the church recalls what at times has been forgotten: that Christianity is first and foremost a lay movement supported by the trained and committed leadership of clergy and laity alike.

NOTES

1. *The Interpreter's Dictionary of the Bible,* vol. 2 (Nashville: Abingdon Press, 1962), 240.
2. *The Book of Concord: The Confessions of the Evangelical Lutheran Church,* Robert Kolb and Timothy J. Wengert, eds. (Minneapolis: Fortress Press, 2000), 406.

CHAPTER THREE

Principle 1—The Relational Church Frog: Faith is formed through personal, trusted relationships

Lily Pad Roots: How does faith happen in the lives of people?

A variety of biblical texts can be used to discuss how people become people of faith. Basically, such belongs to the work of the Holy Spirit (John 20:21-23; 1 Corinthians 12:3) and the role of baptism (John 3:1-8; Acts 2:37-42; Romans 6:1-4). Paul states it succinctly when he writes, ". . . faith comes from what is heard, and what is heard comes through the word of Christ" (Romans 10:17). The Christian community can speak of faith as the result of what God does for us as a gift (2 Corinthians 5:17-18; Ephesians 2:8). And yet, questions still remain:

- How does God reach out to us, create faith in us, and call us to be a unique people of God?
- How is it that the Holy Spirit touches people's lives?

During the Reformation, Martin Luther asked such questions in his treatise on the Magnificat.[1] He wanted to know what the "school" of the Holy Spirit was. Luther understood human experience as the classroom of the Holy Spirit. It is not enough to be given correct doctrine to believe and follow. Somehow the content of the faith needs a context that makes it both believable and understandable. Luther understood Mary, the mother of Jesus, as the prototype Christian, and her words, "Let it be with me according to your word" (Luke 1:38), as the model for the Christian life and faith.

Further, Luther understood Mary to be speaking "on the basis of her own experience, in which she was enlightened and instructed by the Holy Spirit" in the hymn of praise in Luke 1.[2] According to Luther, God and God's word are understood only through the Holy Spirit, and the medium for instruction, or the school for the Spirit of God, is "experiencing, proving, and feeling" the word of God.[3] With this experience of God that recognizes how God helps "only the poor, despised, afflicted, miserable, forsaken, and those who are nothing," the individual is moved to respond with unrestrained joy.[4] Such a response is filled with praise that cannot be taught with words alone but "must be learned in one's own experience," as was the case with Mary. She magnified God in her own soul, with her whole being that was overcome with joy through the work of God.[5]

Pivotal for Luther is the conviction that one is not saved by what God does for another person but only by what God does for each particular individual.[6] Therefore, the experience, the feelings, the praise must be a part of one's own life and not that borrowed from another. Mary's own experience is shared to indicate how God means to work in all lives. It is this learning through words and personal experience that allows us to understand the works of God, which, according to Luther, are the true art of life.[7] Luther writes,

> Unless we learn and experience these works of God, there will be no service of God, no Israel, no grace, no mercy, no God, though we kill ourselves with singing and ringing in the churches and drag into them all the goods in all the world.[8]

The art of life is not in the singing of the Magnificat, but in experiencing and living the Magnificat.

The point of asking and exploring how one comes to have faith is to help the church understand how God chooses to work in the world. For our purposes, the focus is how God uses God's people as instruments of grace, as "stewards of God's mysteries" (1 Corinthians 4:1). Here is one of the great mysteries of faith: God uses fallible creatures like us to do God's work and will in the world. This insight can help church leaders and the entire body of Christ share Christ and nurture faith in one another.

Tadpole Tales: Meet some church frogs

For years we have asked groups of Christians in parenting or Sunday morning education classes, or lay and clergy leaders in workshops, training sessions, or retreats, "Who or what has influenced your life of faith?" In one group of about 50 adults in a Sunday morning forum, the first answer placed on the chalkboard was "mother." The second was "father." The third, "grandparent," and then "godparent." Other answers that were added included the birth of a child, the death of a loved one, the witness of other friends and family, and the experience of being in a war.

When asked for impressions or conclusions that could be drawn from the list on the board, people responded by saying things like, "Family is clearly important," or, "The focus seems to be on relationships," or, "Personal experiences seem to have a role to play." These observations are consistent with formal research on the topic. Youth from seventh to twelfth grades were asked this same question. The number one and two answers *they* gave were "mother" and "father." When adults were asked this question, their responses included spouse (men especially mentioned spouse as a factor).

INFLUENCE	PERCENTAGE CHOOSING AS 1 OF TOP 5			
Mother	Female	74 %	Male	81%
Father	Female	50%	Male	61%
Pastor	Female	44%	Male	57%
Grandparent	Female	29%	Male	30%
Youth group	Female	30%	Male	30%
Christian education	Female	26%	Male	26%
Bible	Female	24%	Male	25%
Friends	Female	29%	Male	22%
Church school teacher	Female	21%	Male	26%
Church camp	Female	28%	Male	20%
Youth group leader	Female	16%	Male	15%
Movie/music star	Female	3%	Male	4%
Revivals/rallies	Female	4%	Male	3%

Percentages reflect an average score of seventh through twelfth graders.[9]

Not everyone was excited by the conclusions that were drawn. One man who appeared to be in his late 50s or early 60s asked with a pained look on his face, "Why didn't anyone mention the church?" When asked what he meant by that question, he said, "Why didn't anyone mention Sunday school, confirmation class, or the youth league?"

Two conclusions arose from the man's question. First, it was revealing that after all the answers on the board were reviewed, not one of those answers mentioned such traditional programs of the church as Sunday school, confirmation class, or youth groups. This is especially worth noting since the respondents represented a biased population.

These were adults who were present at worship as well as at Christian education in the congregation. They were likely to be more supportive of congregational activities like worship and Christian education than those in the congregation not present at the adult forum, or other adults who consider themselves Christian and yet are not active—or even members—in a congregation.

The second conclusion drawn from these conversations, however, was that the list on the board *did*, in fact, reflect the church. The church, people acknowledged, is more than programs designed by congregational leaders—both professional staff and volunteers. The church includes neighbors, friends, new acquaintances, parents, grandparents, godparents, uncles, aunts, and others who care about the faith life of children, youth, and adults in a variety of settings. The church is "a holy nation," the people of God who are called out of darkness and into God's marvelous light with the task of sharing the good news of Jesus Christ (see 1 Peter 2:9).

The church teaches and preaches that this is its very essence and nature, and yet, as we have said, the way the church operates tends to suggest that the real church can be reduced to what takes place at a certain facility, at specified times, and preferably with a pastor present. The man's question, "Why didn't anyone mention the church?" reflected a Christian theology that developed out of an experience of being part of the institutional, public life of the church. "Church" had come to be limited to things like Sunday school, confirmation class, youth group, and, it is safe to add, corporate worship. Interestingly, he himself had not mentioned any of these programmatic experiences of church. It is likely that he, too, had a larger experience of church through family, other personal relationships, and memorable experiences beyond the walls of a congregation. But those experiences were not reinforced by the institution as something to be valued as "church."

One could interpret this story as a critique of all things institutional, but our point is to advocate for a balance between corporate institutional structures and relational ministry in the public and domestic settings. In fact the public structures of church bind our faith in daily life experiences. Good preaching, teaching, worship, and fellowship in the congregational setting routinely feed the faith life in the home. The corporate life of faith was immediately drawn upon following the September 11th attacks on the World Trade Center, Pentagon, and the four hijacked airplanes, for example. Mourners gathered together in congregational settings across the country in large numbers. They found solace in worship and the fellowship of one another.

Tadpole Tale: The importance of care

Another important conclusion can be drawn from the people or events named as influences on the faith life of people. When a clergyperson is mentioned, his or her relational abilities, not preaching and teaching, are the primary reason. One woman identified her youth pastor as an important influence in her faith life. When asked if his preaching and teaching were influential, she responded, "I don't think those were his gifts." When pressed to name how he was a factor in her faith journey, the woman simply said, "He cared." She then went on to describe how the pastor had been an important support for her family during her years in high school when her father lost his job.

Another example of this kind of personal influence from a pastor came from a male youth director who identified the pastor at his parochial elementary school. Again, this man was asked if the influence was due to the pastor's preaching and teaching. The man said, "No. He taught me a fall-away jump shot on the basketball court." The youth director then described how he had experienced a difficult family history as a young child and was orphaned at an early age. While searching for a place to belong, he found a powerful level of acceptance and warmth from a pastor on a basketball court.

Even when the preaching and teaching ministry of a clergyperson is noted, it is often associated with the recollection of a personal, trusted relationship with the pastor. Clear evidence exists of preaching in the church that is superbly edifying and inspiring, and the recollection of personal relationships remembered by parishioners is not meant to slight the proclamation of the gospel. However, it appears that often it is not the edifying, inspiring Word *alone* that brings the message home, but the living Word presented in the context of a trusted relationship.

One older gentleman told a story of his pastor. The man's wife was in the hospital in critical condition and he and his family spent a long night waiting for his wife to get out of surgery. The man's pastor spent the night with him and his family in the hospital waiting room. When morning came, the husband learned that his wife would be okay. As the man tells it, he was convinced that his pastor would never again preach a bad sermon because he experienced an individual who cared enough to spend a long night in the hospital to support a family in crisis.

One woman, who emigrated from eastern Europe to the United States after World War II, identified her pastor's preaching and adult confirmation training as influential in her life of faith. When asked what about his preaching was edifying, she noted that her pastor used big words in his sermons. She listened to his sermons and wrote down some of his words. When she got home after the Sunday service, she got out her dictionary and learned new English words. She also pointed out how the pastor and his wife had taken a personal interest in her and her transition to the American culture. They had personally helped her get a new start in a new country. She was truly devoted to this couple, his pastoral ministry, and their church.

Tadpole Tale: From booth to pew

One of our favorite stories is about a friend of ours, a pastor in a midsize, midwestern community. One day, he was sitting in a local fast food restaurant at about 3:00 P.M. eating a hamburger. Across the street from the restaurant, the local high school emptied out. The restaurant quickly filled up with hungry teenagers. Five imposing and threatening young men circled our friend's booth. One of them had a lock and chain around his neck (literally, a towing chain and a padlock). This young man got into the face of our friend and said, "Hey man, you're in our booth." Not wanting trouble, our friend began to slide out of the booth. Behind "Ol' Lock and Chains" and his posse, a teenager stepped forward and said, "Pastor, what are you doing here?" This teen was a member of his congregation. Our friend quickly explained that he was eating his hamburger and now needs to be on his way. Suddenly, Lock and Chains looked at our friend and asked, "You a pastor?" He shoved our friend back into the booth and the whole group of five guys slid in around him. He was trapped with ketchup running down his tie from the hamburger now pressed up against his chest. Lock and Chains said, "Tell me pastor, what do you think of the devil?" Our friend paused, considered his situation and then said, "Oh, I don't know; what do you think?" Lock and Chains responded, "Well, I think he sucks!" Our friend gleefully said, "Me too!!" What happened next was amazing. For the next 90 minutes, our friend led a Bible study on the problem of evil in the world! Lock and Chains and his posse were deeply interested in this spiritual question. The booth had become a pew.

At the end of their time together, Lock and Chains turned to him one more time. "What do think of this Revelation sh--?" he asked. Our friend said, "Let's meet here next week and talk about it." He soon began running Bible studies every Wednesday from this fast food pew. Our friend had established some real credibility with this unorthodox group and continued to build powerful relationships with them.

These and other stories like them are not intended to suggest that Christian evangelism can be reduced to establishing "warm and fuzzy" feelings with people. These examples do indicate, however, that in the context of personal, trusted relationships—often those in one's own home or some other non-congregational setting—people are more receptive to the Christian faith. Such experiences become the work of the Holy Spirit through which people are "experiencing, proving, and feeling" the word of God.

Tadpole Tale: Cross-cultural examples

Such faith-forming experiences are not confined to the North American context. A Presbyterian pastor from Nigeria says that to learn about the development of the Christian faith in his national context, one must "listen to the elders," that is, one must pay attention to the older lay leaders who have stories of the faith to tell, which nurture the young. Many of those elders are the grandmothers and grandfathers of the community.

Benjamin Ngede, a Christian educator in Tanzania, shares a similar perspective. He has studied the community life and the stories of the Christian communities in his country in order to help the new generations pass on the Christian faith. His concern has been the loss of the role of village elders. When the missionaries from Europe came to Africa in the eighteenth and nineteenth centuries, the model of church that they brought with them at times undermined the communal structures already in existence. Christianity was transmitted to people in Tanzania in a way that made the people dependent upon the pastor to the exclusion of the storytelling and spiritual role of the elders. Ngede is seeking to recover the indigenous methods of passing on faith and values that had sustained his people for centuries.

In Upsala, Sweden, church leaders in the areas of children's ministry, youth ministry, and family ministry were brought together to study the principles and strategies presented in this book. They were asked to identify a person or an event that had significantly influenced their Christian faith. Of the 14 people who were present for that exercise, eight mentioned grandmothers, grandfathers, or both. Again, this is a biased population—people who have invested their lives vocationally in the Church of Sweden. One would think that these church leaders would have identified the preaching, teaching, or worship life of the church as the chief influences in their faith. Yet, they too could not overlook how their faith had been significantly shaped by the personal, trusted relationship of a grandparent, an elder who spoke and acted in such a way that helped pass on the Christian faith to the next generation.

Andrew Hsao, church historian and former president of a seminary in Hong Kong, studied the development of the Christian faith in China. He notes that Christianity and Buddhism both had a foothold in China in the seventh century,[10] but concludes that Buddhism won out over Christianity in no small measure due to the domestic nature of Buddhism. The Buddhist family had a shrine for worship in the home. Christians, however, were more likely to leave their dwellings to gather together in a sanctuary. For years, Hsao interviewed all new students from the People's Republic of China who entered the seminary. He would ask them how it was that they became Christians in a communist land. The consistent answer he received was the influence of their families—mothers and fathers, grandmothers and grandfathers. This interview process led Hsao to conclude that the family in communist China is the first "seminary" of the church.

Mindaugas Sabutis from Vilnius, Lithuania, a pastor in the Lithuanian Evangelical Lutheran Church, attended a Youth and Family Certification School in California sponsored by the Center for Youth Ministries of Wartburg Seminary in Dubuque, Iowa. During the three-week school, he shared the history of his church in Lithuania. Of the four million people in Lithuania, 80 percent are Roman Catholic. The other Christian groups are largely divided among the Russian Orthodox, Lutherans, and the Reformed. Prior to World War II there were 250,000 Lutherans, but after the war and the occupation by the Soviet Union, the numbers dropped to 30,000. Many Lutherans experienced discrimination by the government in Lithuania because they were associated with its German heritage, and therefore were perceived as potential Nazi sympathizers.

Sabutis pointed out that a critical moment in the history of Lithuanian Lutheranism was the development of pietism, which gained its ascendancy in Lithuania during the late nineteenth century. Pietism was a lay movement that had strong pastoral support and participation. The focus of pietism is the gathering of Christians in homes for preaching, hymn singing, and prayers. Services could last for hours and might be led by lay persons or clergy. Pietistic homes would use books of lengthy sermons called home postils written by Jacob Philip Spener or Hermann Franke, the founders of Lutheran pietism. The father would read these home postils to the entire family on Sundays when they were not able to travel to a Lutheran congregation for worship. Cards with Bible and hymn verses would also be used in the homes to sustain the Christian families during the week.

Since many Lutherans lived on farms away from the cities, this form of worship and faith formation was a key factor in passing on the faith to the next generations.

The pietistic tradition was vitally important to Lithuanian Lutherans during Soviet and German occupation in World War II, and the Soviet occupation that followed. Only a handful of Lutheran churches remained open between 1945 and 1990, but behind closed doors in the homes, Lutherans continued to teach the faith using Luther's Small Catechism, the Bible, hymnbooks, prayer books, and home postils. After the collapse of the Soviet Union, the Lithuanian people returned to the churches *en masse*, and the general population was surprised to learn of the presence of the Lutheran church, which had continued as a clandestine religious group for more than five decades.

The indigenous people of Central and South America have long experienced oppression at the hands of the landed aristocracies, whose roots are in Europe. Catholicism has historically had the difficult challenge of choosing between support for the poor, indigenous people, or identifying with the aristocracy. In recent decades, Catholic priests and nuns have taken great steps to advocate for the economic, political, social, and spiritual lives of the native populations. One of the means to this social revolution has been the development of the Christian base community—small groups of Christians that gather for Bible study, prayer, and works of loving service. These communities have had a major influence in the lives of the indigenous peoples throughout Central and South America.

Throughout church history and around the globe, numerous examples of the impact of the domestic church are evident. Personal, trusted relationships are a central means through which the Holy Spirit touches peoples' lives.

Lily Pad Roots: A view from the history of religion

Religious sociologist Rodney Stark conducted interdisciplinary research and drew similar conclusions. His goal was to understand why Christianity rose so quickly and became the official religion in the Roman Empire by the time of Constantine in A.D. 325. Comparing a variety of religious groups, Stark discovered that "conversion tends to proceed along social networks formed by interpersonal attachments."[11] The Mormon experience illustrates this conclusion well. Stark noted that for every thousand cold calls that a Mormon missionary makes, on average, one convert is made. Stark continues, "However, when missionaries make their first contact with a person in the home of a Mormon friend or relative of that person, this results in conversion 50 percent of the time."[12]

This "friends and family" formula worked in the first centuries of Christianity as well. Stark estimates that the early church grew at a rate of 40 percent a decade (a pattern matched by Mormons in the twentieth century). Stark offers persuasive evidence to indicate that Christianity grew, in part, through the network system of the *hellenized* (Greek) Jews of the Diaspora. Early Christian missionaries, often hellenized Jews themselves, benefited from the "family and friendship connections within some of the Diaspora communities."[13] In addition, Stark notes the importance of caring hospitality in witnessing to Jesus. The church developed in the context of a variety of plagues sweeping through the Roman Empire. The standard practice among Romans was to abandon those who were sick, but Christians exercised simple nursing care for those infected by smallpox, measles, and other diseases. Without any understanding of the development of immunity, this simple nursing care helped two out of three in their care survive the plague. Christianity exponentially grew because of this hospitality, and Christians became known as effective healers. Such simple practices transformed Roman cities like Alexandria into centers of Christianity.[14]

Lily Pad Roots: Faith formed through personal relationships— some New Testament themes

Faith formed through personal relationships is clearly an evangelical perspective that is present in the New Testament. First Thessalonians is considered by many to be the oldest book of the New Testament. In this letter, Paul seeks to support and guide a nascent Christian community. However, Paul does not see his primary tool to be the theological insights he disseminates in the letter, but rather a longing to be with the community "face to face and restore what is lacking in [their] faith" (Thessalonians 3:10; see also 2:1, and Colossians 2:17). In lieu of his absence from the Thessalonians, Paul sent Timothy to Thessalonica "to strengthen and encourage you for the sake of your faith" (1 Thessalonians 3:2). Paul sent someone else to be with the Thessalonians "face-to-face." Paul operates with the understanding that teaching the faith is not merely a matter of giving correct doctrinal and ethical answers. The Christian nurture that Paul is seeking requires personal, trusted, face-to-face contact.

In this same letter, Paul likens each missionary to the Thessalonians as a breast-feeding nurse caring for her children (1 Thessalonians 2:7), or as a father exhorting his children (2:11-12). The language and imagery that Paul uses to describe the nurturing relationship between a group of missionaries and a young congregation is personal, relational, intimate, and familial.

Jesus himself had his own fellowship of trusted followers. He called them by name, personally invited them to follow, and considered them family. He sent them out in pairs to heal the sick and to share the message of the kingdom with individual households from village to village. When those households extended hospitality to Jesus' disciples and received them, the disciples were to bless the household. When the disciples' presence was shunned, they went on to other dwellings and other villages (see Matthew 10:5-15; Mark 6: 7-13; Luke 9:1-6; 10:1-12).

Jesus is often remembered for his ministry in the midst of throngs of people, for example, the Sermon on the Mount, the triumphant entry into Jerusalem, and the feedings of the multitudes. But these dramatic episodes in Jesus' ministry often overshadow Jesus' typical encounters with people in small groups. Even some of the large gatherings with Jesus happened at times when he was attempting to get away and be alone for prayer or fellowship with his small group of disciples.

Numerous narratives of Jesus in more intimate settings exist. He visits the homes of religious leaders (Simon, the Pharisee), a social outcast (Zacchaeus), sisters (Mary and Martha), and Peter's mother. He meets people on his journeys and heals them or their loved ones (the 10 lepers, a man born blind, the woman with the flow of blood, the man with an epileptic son, the centurion's slave). He taught his disciples in a small fishing boat on the Sea of Galilee. He taught the Pharisee, Nicodemus, alone in the middle of the night. He takes only three of his disciples with him to the Mount of Transfiguration. Abundant evidence exists of faith formed through personal contact, and through the development of personal relationships in Jesus' ministry. His ministry had legs to get to people far beyond the arena of synagogue and Temple.

Lily Pad Roots: Evangelism 101
Faith formed through personal, trusted relationships

The Gospel of John offers another example of the role of personal relationships in serving the ministry and testimony of the church. In the first chapter, John the Baptist identifies Jesus with the words "Here is the Lamb of God who takes away the sin of the world!" (1:29). A second time John identifies Jesus in similar words (1:36). Two disciples of John the Baptist hear this testimony and, as trusting followers of John the Baptist, begin to follow Jesus. Jesus asks the two disciples of John, "What are you looking for?" Their response to his inquiry is revealing. They simply ask, "Where are you staying?" (1:38). They do not ask for truth or wisdom or salvation or answers to philosophical or theological problems. They first want to establish a relationship with Jesus. They want to know where Jesus is staying, where he is lodging.

The verb to stay or to *dwell* is significant in the Gospel of John. To stay, lodge, dwell, remain, or abide all are translations of the Greek word *meno* used in John 1:38. To be a follower of Jesus is to dwell with Jesus and have a relationship with Jesus, just as Jesus dwells with God the Father, the Spirit of God dwells with Jesus (John 1:32-33), and the Father abides in Jesus (14:10). Those who are followers of Jesus have a relationship with God the Father and the Holy Spirit through their relationship with Jesus.

The importance of the two disciples wanting to know where Jesus dwells (John 1:38) soon becomes evident. Jesus responds to their question with the invitation to discover where he is staying. He simply says, "Come and see" (1:39). Jesus does not pull out his electronic daily planner in order that the disciples of John might have the opportunity to schedule an appointment with Jesus at some future point in time. He leaves no suggestion that they should leave a voice mail message, contact him by e-mail, or find the Jesus Web site. Rather, Jesus extends an immediate and open invitation; a gesture of open hospitality: "Y'all come . . . and come now." Jesus accepts their desire to have ongoing, personal contact with him as the means by which these new followers will grow in their understanding of who Jesus is and what his life means to them.

One of the two disciples is Andrew, who quickly finds his brother Simon, says to him, "We have found the Messiah," and brings him to Jesus (John 1:41). Another disciple is now incorporated into Jesus' growing community. It happens through an invitation and introduction made by a brother. Once again, faith is formed through personal, trusted relationships, this time through a sibling. Then Jesus calls Philip to follow him.

Interestingly, the only description given about Philip is that he is from Bethsaida, the same city as Andrew and Peter (Simon). Bethsaida is not a Roman or even Judean metropolitan center, but a community where people most likely knew each other's families and each other's names and faces. Andrew, Peter, and Philip are neighborhood boys. Here it is easy to imagine faith formed through personal, trusted relationships, and this time, through relationships formed through childhood instruction (school), games (soccer practices), and being in each other's homes (hospitality).

Still in the first chapter of John, Philip seeks out Nathanael, someone who is apparently a friend of his. Philip bears testimony to Jesus, but Nathanael is skeptical. Philip simply responds with the kind of exhortation and invitation that Jesus used earlier: "Come and see" (1:46). The implication is that Nathanael could find the truth for himself. This is not heavy-handed evangelism, but suggests a spirit of hospitality, openness, and welcome.

These texts from John present critical understandings regarding evangelism for the church today. First, the phrase "come and see" is expressed through various Greek words in the Johannine texts. This suggests that it is not important to have a memorized script to share the message of Christ. The point may simply be that the ideas of invitation and hospitality are critical to the evangelistic task. Second, when the woman at the well wonders if Jesus could be the Messiah, the Greek phrasing of her question implies that she does not think he is. The marvel of her conversation with the Samaritans is that even this very modest and doubtful endorsement is enough to introduce faith in Christ to these people. Evangelism is first and foremost *God's* work, and the story of the woman at the well demonstrates that God can and does work through human wonderment and doubt to create faith. This is clearly a word of encouragement for twenty-first century western Christians who tend to be fearful of offending others with deep convictions. The woman at the well presents anything but that kind of certainty.

An astonishingly simple and effective method of evangelism is presented in the Gospel of John. What was begun through personal relationship and invitation ("come and see") results in a confession of faith made by those who had not previously known Jesus as Messiah (1:41), the one written about by the law and the prophets (1:45), the Son of God (1:49), the Savior (4:42).

Tadpole Tale: Anywhere but here

When this approach to evangelization and faith nurture was introduced to seminary students in Lund, Sweden, one student offered her critique after class: "That was a very interesting lecture," she said, "but it's different here in Sweden." (This is not a unique reaction. We hear it in our own country, too. When in the Pacific Northwest or in the South, we hear the caution, "It is different here in _____.") The woman explained her resistance to this concept. She shared that socialist (read: communist) parents raised her and gave her a Russian name, Katinka, instead of a Swedish name to memorialize in her life their economic, political, and religious (atheistic) ideals. Yet, to help her grow up to be a moral, global citizen, they placed her in a Roman Catholic day care center at age three. It was there that Katinka was introduced to Christ.

We asked Katinka if there were people at the day care center with whom she developed a personal, trusted relationship. She immediately said, "Oh yes, there was Sister Bernarda and Sister Ansgari." Then we asked what it was about them that was so meaningful. Again without hesitation—in fact, with great delight—Katinka said, "Well, each day when I arrived at the school, they greeted me and hugged me; they played with me, prayed with me, placed me on their laps."

At that moment you could see it in Katinka's eyes. She got it: faith is formed by the power of the Holy Spirit through personal trusted relationships, often—but not always— in our own homes. Her tone, facial expressions, and direction of conversation changed dramatically. She mused, "You know, now that I work in the church, my parents sometimes come to church to see me up front." One more time she heard the words, "Faith is formed through personal, trusted relationships, often in our own homes." This time she also heard, "and sometimes a child shall lead them."

Croaks, Ribbits, and Hops

How people use the term *church* has great impact on expectations, hopes, and ways of behaving as the people of God in Christ. The word can be described in very lofty, theological terms, in personal experiential terms, and in ways that are shaped by the programs and activities of a local congregation. A primary goal of this book is to broaden our perception of how God reaches out to us in daily life and how the body of Christ is at work in the world.

Explore the following questions alone or, better yet, with others:
- Who or what has influenced your life of faith?
- What does all of this say about how you define the word *church?*

As fundamental and as obvious as it may seem, the relational nature of faith, values, and character formation is often overlooked in our fast-paced society. Time and attention needs to be given to simple ways to make life a bit more bearable and relationships a bit more central to our lives. Such prioritizing can positively impact personal well-being, family life, friendship ties, and even the ministry of the church.

Memorable occasions for families include mealtimes, vacations, and time spent together in nature.
- What are some favorite memories of time spent together with family and friends?

- What are some memorable patterns from the past that you have not done for some time?
- Think of memory-making and relationship-bonding moments that could be introduced or reintroduced into your family life. Make a pledge to act on one or more of these ideas.

Sometimes adults get frustrated with the pace of life and the loss of a dinner hour together. Too many dinners are eaten alone, on the run, or in front of a television set. One particular family made family dinner time a high priority. On occasions when time was especially short, they would buy fast food and bring it home. But then they would take the food out of the restaurant wrappers and place it on elegant dishes to make the mealtime a bit more special.

- What ideas can you imagine to make mealtime a special time of day with others (especially if you live alone)?

An important beginning point for Christian discipleship and evangelism is the simple gesture of welcoming other people. The Scriptures show high regard for this form of kindness. Hebrews 13:2 states, "Do not neglect to show hospitality to strangers, for by doing that some have entertained angels without knowing it." This text could easily be alluding to the three strangers, who visited aged Abraham and Sarah by the oaks of Mamre and announced that they would be the parents of their own child (Genesis 18:1-15). The immediate context in Hebrews is the need to show hospitality to Christians from other areas, some of whom were missionaries of the gospel.

- Consider ways to extend hospitality to others, including strangers. U.S. society has largely lost the art of showing hospitality. For example, if you are at someone's home the television may be kept on or a stereo may not be turned down to conversational levels. Offering a guest something to eat or drink has, for some, become a lost gesture.

The very idea of inviting someone into a home is often neglected because of the embarrassment of a home that is not quite tidy enough. Hospitality may be a Christian trait that needs renewed attention. Basic skills of hospitality need to be taught to many whom have not experienced this rudimentary act of kindness.

- What are some basic gestures of hospitality that seem to have been lost by many in today's society?
- Are there some that you have overlooked in recent times?

- Be specific and decide what correctives or additions you might bring into your own home to act on the Christian ethic of hospitality.

A couple had a very gregarious teen that spent many evenings away from home with her friends. One evening on one of those rather rare occasions when the group of teens was at their home, the parents stated how they would like to see the youth more in their home; that they wanted them to feel welcomed and to spend more time in a home rather than being at coffee houses and restaurants so much. The parents asked the teens to write down the foods they liked for snacks and promised to make sure the snack foods (including non-alcoholic drinks) would be available to the youth whenever they came over. The youth were quick to comply with the request. At the end of the list written by the youth was added, "P.S. Dear Jack and Cheryl, we love you." It was an added message that touched the couple very deeply.

- What initiatives can you image that would help others feel welcomed in your home?
- Can you, with good, ethical safeguards, make your home a place where teens are welcome?
- What steps would you take to do this?

The experiential dimension of faith formation includes our cultural experiences.
- What contact have you had with Christians from another culture?
- What have you learned from them about how they understand and live their faith that might enrich your own faith journey?

The theme of this chapter has been "faith is formed through the power of the Holy Spirit through personal, trusted relationships—often relationships in our own homes." Remember the Swedish woman who said that it was different in her culture?
- What issues might be leading you to say, "Yes, but it is different here"?
- List them and keep them in mind as you read the rest of this book. Be open to how your questions may be answered later in the book or how those questions may simply take on important, ongoing significance.

All the suggested *croaks, ribbits, and hops* have congregational as well as personal applications. Consider the *croaks, ribbits, and hops* from the perspective of a local congregation.
- How could the congregation take an active role in helping to explore and respond to these issues?

NOTES

1. *Luther's Works,* vol. 21, Jaroslav Pelikan, ed., (St. Louis: Concordia Publishing House, 1956), 229, 300, 350.
2. Ibid., 299.
3. Ibid., 299.
4. Ibid., 300.
5. Ibid., 307.
6. Ibid., 318.
7. Ibid., 331.
8. Ibid., 350.
9. Unpublished data from research for *Effective Christian Education: A National Study of Protestant Congregations* (Minneapolis: Search Institute, 1990). Used with permission.
10. See "Did Christianity Thrive in China?" Bay Fang, *U.S. News & World Report,* March 5, 2001, 51.
11. Rodney Stark, *The Rise of Christianity: How the Obscure, Marginal Jesus Movement Became the Dominant Religious Force in the Western World in a Few Centuries* (San Francisco: Harper Collins, 1996), 18.
12. Ibid., 18.
13. Ibid., 62.
14. Ibid., 75.

CHAPTER FOUR

Principle 2—The Total Church Frog: The Church is a Living Partnership between Home and Congregation

Congregations are searching. They are experimenting with new ways of reaching members, visitors, and communities with the gospel. The motivation derives from frustration with declining or plateaued membership, enthusiasm that certain strategies have been working and more can still be done, or some combination of both. Congregations often engage in the search for effective ministry by soliciting the experience or expertise of leadership from neighboring congregations, denominational staff, or outside church consultants.

No matter who is brought in to assist, a common assumption made by nearly all such helpers is that effective ministry has to do with the programs and activities of the local congregation. Primary attention rests on what takes place on the premises of the congregation, and after months—if not years—of congregational meetings, assessments of needs, and diagnoses of problems, the recommendations are remarkably the same: more exciting worship, more exciting youth ministry, and a larger parking lot.

Sometimes a fourth strategy is to have more road signs and advertisements directing people to the congregation. By the time these not-so-novel conclusions have been drawn, congregations are broke from the financial investments, and the leadership is often too worn out to do anything with the results. Another congregational plan ends up shelved and little happens to enliven the congregation's ministry.

The assumption that effective ministry is exclusively about congregational programs and activities exacerbates the crisis of congregational ministry. Faithful, healthy, and effective congregational ministry does not only entail attention to church frog heads (congregational leadership) and church frog torsos (the congregation gathered together for worship, education, fellowship, and service). Church frog legs (Christians living and serving in the midst of daily routines outside the congregational setting) have been generally ignored—or severely limited—in the endeavor to develop new ministry models, statements, and plans.

The result is only to make things worse. Pastors, other leaders, and the programs of the congregation have been asked to impact the lives and faith of individuals in ways that go beyond their capacities. Too many ministry eggs have been placed in the congregational basket. A congregation, like the rest of creation, is broken and sinful. In the best of circumstances it will never accomplish all that we ask of it. At the same time, the congregation has been burdened with goals and tasks that are more than unreasonable. No magic Sunday school curriculum, confirmation program, youth group, seniors group, or golden-tongued preacher will suffice to turn ministry around and satisfy everyone's needs and wishes.

When parishioners complain that the pastor's sermon didn't feed their spirits, the hymns were not the best choices, or the congregation's focus for outreach is misplaced, one reasonable response is, "So what?!" Of course, congregations want to be sensitive and make wise choices and lead faithfully from the pulpit, altar, choir loft, and committee rooms, but making all the right choices and doing all the right things will never happen this side of the kingdom yet to come. Sometime, somewhere, someone has to say to people who complain about poor sermons, hymns, and service projects, "Tough!" If you don't like the sermon, go home and preach the one you needed to hear. If you don't like the hymns, go home and sing the ones you like. If you don't like where the congregation is spending its time and money in outreach and service, spend your time and money in the areas that you believe need attention. No one is stopping you. Congregational members will never totally agree on anything, and if we wait until they do, very little will ever happen in the congregation to live out the prayer, "Your kingdom come, Your will be done."

Congregations that are doing meaningful ministry in local communities and beyond tend to be those that understand the balance between the ministry of the congregation and the ministry that extends from apartments, houses, duplexes, and anywhere else where Christians dwell. The front doors to the ministry of a local congregation are doors that are often located far away from the congregational facilities; they are the doors that open to homes, coffee houses, grocery stores, and other places where people meet, greet, and invite one another to "come and see" Jesus.

Tadpole Tale: The church that disappoints

A pastor's elderly parents moved into a townhouse complex where many of the residents were also senior citizens. Shortly after their move to the new home, the son drove his parents to the congregation that they planned to join. The son wanted to make sure the congregation was aware of his parents' move to the area and their needs for community and spiritual support. The congregation's reputation for a large and active seniors group already pleased the family. The son and the parents sat down with one of the congregation's pastors and the son explained that his parents were new to the area and were planning to join the congregation. He also explained to the pastor that his parents both had health needs and a need for congregational support.

Through casual introductions at the townhouse complex, the pastor's parents met the president of the seniors' group. The woman was actually a neighbor in the complex. But although the couple introduced themselves to the seniors' group president and explained their interest in the congregation, and although a pastor had a personal, face-to-face visit with the couple, and the couple worshiped at the congregation a few times, no invitations were ever made to join a seniors' group gathering, no knocks were made on their door, no phone calls came, no letters were sent, no personal greetings were given. The mother was already dealing with depression (a point shared with the congregational pastor). Her conclusion was that even God had given up on her. She and her husband never did join the congregation.

The irony is that this is a congregation very aware of the need for and importance of outreach. They advertise in the community a number of different ways, including a very visible advertisement that is displayed before the beginning of movies at a major movie theater complex located in the community. Here is a good example of a large, growth-conscious congregation that understands that community visibility is important and works at ways to promote large-scale attendance at its worship services and ministries like the senior citizens group. But, the congregation is not as aware that the ministry of the congregation extends through neighborly contacts as well. The pastor, likely very busy with meetings and trying to find ways to expand the ministry of the congregation, could not find the time—or simply did not remember—to contact the elderly couple or suggest that someone else make contact. The president of the seniors' group may be a popular and effective leader of group gatherings, but did not perceive the important ministry of reaching out to people who live only doors away but are not at the senior functions. The front door to the ministry of that congregation could have been at a townhouse porch. The "front door" could have even been a phone call from one home to another.

Lily Pad Roots: The home as the church outside the walls

The ministry of the church is often informal and not associated with congregational committees or staff. Jesus' own ministry took place along roads, on beaches, in homes, as well as in synagogues or the Temple. The church began with an itinerant preacher and his followers. Since that time, the work of the church has always involved the spiritual gifts and faith of Christians who did not attend Sunday school, never finished confirmation, avoided church committees and boards, and sometimes were never regular participants at weekly worship. The work of the church has been and continues to be a living partnership between the ministry of the congregation and the ministry of people outside the congregation, people like shepherds in a field near Bethlehem, Zacchaeus, a woman with a flow of blood who sought healing wherever she could find it, a woman at the well at Sychar, and anyone's Uncle Lenny. The church is not restricted to ministry for people who enter through the doors into a church building.

The reference to "home" in this chapter refers to any social contact that takes place in the daily lives of people. "When you are at home or when you are away [from home]" (Deuteronomy 6:7), is a biblical image for the life of God's faithful people wherever they are. It is an image that recognizes the faith-formative influence of time and relationships in the home in the daily lives of the faithful. This is a setting located outside the walls of the temple, the synagogue, or church building, and represents an environment essential to, yet other than, life in the institutionally-sanctioned Christian fellowship. Both environments are vital.

Lily Pad Roots: It has been like this from the beginning

From the beginning of the life of the church in the New Testament, the partnership between home and congregation, or home and the public worship setting has been the norm. Acts 2 provides a description of the beginning of the church at Pentecost. The disciples were gathered together in a house in Jerusalem, and the Holy Spirit came upon them. By the power of the Holy Spirit the disciples began to speak in foreign languages that could be understood by the Jews who had been gathered in

Jerusalem from "every nation under heaven" (Acts 2:5). The Jews had come for the Jewish festival of Pentecost, the celebration of the giving of the Law seven weeks after Passover. Through the preaching of Peter, these Jews were hearing a new Torah, a new teaching. Three thousand were baptized that day and received the gift of the Holy Spirit.

After a description of this first Christian Pentecost, the life of the church is depicted. The faithful lived together and shared their worldly goods. The distribution of possessions was based on the needs of others. Then the text reads, "Day by day, as they spent much time together in the temple, they broke bread at home and ate their food with glad and generous hearts, praising God and having the goodwill of all the people" (2:46-47). Day by day the first Christians gathered together in the public worship space of the Temple in Jerusalem, and day by day they lived and worshiped from house to house.

The language "broke bread together" is likely a shorthand expression for what is more fully described in Acts 2:42, "They devoted themselves to the apostles' teaching and fellowship, to the breaking of the bread and the prayers." A way of life is described at the beginning of the formation of the church that combines public worship in the Temple and more intimate gatherings in the home. In public and in more personal settings, Christians experienced a way of life that bonded them together as a unique people and edified their life and faith in Christ.

Lily Pad Roots: Three activities

Three distinct activities take place in the partnership between church and home. First is the testimony of Peter, Paul, and the countless others who carry on the ministry given by the Holy Spirit (see Acts 2:4; 9:17; 13:2). This testimony is the gospel of Jesus Christ that has been passed down through the generations from missionaries, pastors, teachers, bishops, elders, and others who have been recognized by the body of Christ. To this day, the church carries on the ministry of proclaiming the gospel publicly through faithful pastors and others who have been trained, supported, and held accountable to the standards of the gospel and the guidance of the Holy Spirit.

The second way in which the church is experienced as a partnership between home and congregation is through the edification from the home that enables the witness, leadership, and service of the larger Christian community. Not only public preaching grew the church, but the "breaking of bread" from house to house. Acts 2 identifies public *and* domestic worship, generosity, and praise that resulted in the good will of all the people and the evangelization of the greater population (2:46-47). Timothy served the larger

Christian community with Paul, his mentor and spiritual father. Paul describes
Timothy's faith as arising out of the faith of his home through his grandmother, Lois,
and mother, Eunice (2 Timothy 1:5-7), and leading to his public ministry. Just as the public ministry of the church builds up individuals and households, so individuals and
households build up the public ministry of the church. The church frog needs the inte-
gration of the whole body. The head and torso need the legs, and the legs need the head
and torso to work together for the good of the church, that is, the body of Christ.

Third, the partnership between home and congregation serves those within and beyond
the body of Christ with interpersonal care. The public church does not merely gather
funds to support individuals and households, but individuals and households support
the larger community of faith (Acts 2:45). At the same time, Christian households reach
out with benevolence that serves those in far away places. For example, Paul gathered
offerings for the church in Jerusalem as he conducted his missionary journeys (Romans
15:25-29; 1 Corinthians 16:1-4), and exhorted the Christians in Galatia to "work for the
good of all, especially for those of the family of faith" (Galatians 6:10). Providential care
is so essential to the life of the Christian, in fact, that the writer of Timothy said, "And
whoever does not provide for relatives, and especially for family members, has denied
the faith and is worse than an unbeliever" (1 Timothy 5:8). Family life is to be protected
and seen as precious, and not to care for the needs of the family is to miss something
central to Christian life and faith. The home provides an arena for building up the body,
and as such, is to be revered and supported.

Lilly Pad Roots: The need for the partnership today

The church in contemporary society has the same need for the vital partnership between home and congregation. In the pluralistic world in which we live,
diverse and contradictory voices can be heard regarding faith, values, and lifestyles. The
public church can serve the life of the home by affirming and reinforcing faithful messages conveyed in the home. Without the elucidation and clarification of the gospel in
the public arena, it can easily be misconstrued or forgotten in the domestic arena. Not
only other world faiths vie for attention in our culture, but perhaps more importantly,
consumerism, prejudice, violence, self-centeredness, and a host of other challenges
seek human allegiance. When a sermon, a lesson in Sunday school, or a caring conversation from a trusted congregational leader rings true to a parent trying to nurture
Christian life and faith in the home, the larger faith community has given its support.
Indeed, the parent trying to raise a child without the larger community certainly has a
difficult path to trod.

This mutuality goes in the other direction as well. The public church speaks wisdom, faith, and love to households, but households also have wisdom, faith, and love to give the public church. The church is always in need of healthy lay leaders to help groom new pastors and other church professionals. The wise pastor knows how to seek out and receive the counsel of elders—those who can help teach the shepherd how to shepherd; and the wise elder realizes how his or her maturity in the faith can be a lasting gift to pastors and the church-at-large. Unfortunately, the current emphasis on professionalism makes it difficult for pastors to be open to the counsel of the laity. Church professionals generally do not enter into the congregational setting looking for church frog legs to provide them with a sturdy foundation for their ministry in the church.

Tadpole Tale: Confirmation guidelines

Many clergy and lay leaders are, in fact, giving more attention to the role of the home in nurturing faith. However, even those who want to make the home a vital place for the ministry of the church often miss the rich possibilities available to them. Parents and other caregivers are valued only in so far as they support the work of the frog head (leadership), or body (public gathering of the church in worship, Christian education, fellowship groups, or service groups). One congregation, for example, informed parents that they were very important to their children's confirmation experience. To help parents effectively support and participate in their children's confirmation program, five specific suggestions were given to parents.

1. Encourage and support your teens in their work. Help them where able, but urge them to give their best.
2. Ensure that your teens have transportation and attend class weekly.
3. Worship regularly with your children.
4. Nurture the importance of stewardship through one's own commitment of time and financial resources.
5. Pray for them and yourselves as they grow and mature.

As helpful and encouraging a list as this is for parents and other primary caregivers of confirmation youth, upon closer examination, one finds that the suggestions do not go far enough to truly partner home and congregation in Christian nurture. Too much emphasis is placed on nurturing faith in the local congregation, and almost nothing promotes the direct contact of teens and adults in the faith journey at home. An analysis of two of these suggestions will illustrate.

The first suggestion seems to emphasize the parent's active participation in the child's faith development, but the "but" in the middle of the sentence undermines real confidence in or support for active involvement. The word *but* serves grammatically by negating what precedes it. Parents should be directly involved, *but* parents generally are not perceived as capable of doing that. The real expectation is that parents should encourage children "to give their best," that is, to remind children of the need to put in the effort. "Go Jeremy, go Kirsten, go Joshua, go Amber. *Don't you have confirmation assignments that are due?*" This assumption severely compromises its intent and leaves the suggestion without much clarity except to tell the child to go away and work alone. In fact, the people responsible for this list re-evaluated it and deleted this recommendation in subsequent years.

Now, the new number one recommendation moved up from number two: being a chauffeur and time manager. The real job of parents or guardians is to bring children "to church," preferably regularly and on time. This recommendation is consistent with how parents feel about their spiritual role. We have asked parents to compare their own understanding of their spiritual role in the home with that of Martin Luther in the sixteenth century. Luther wrote that parents were "apostles, bishops, and priests to their children"[1] (see chapter 3 for further discussion of this theme), but parents today overwhelmingly respond that they feel much too unprepared to have a direct role in their children's faith formation. When asked in what role they do see themselves, the answer is quite consistent, not only in the United States, but in other western countries as well: taxi driver. Parents have learned from the church frog's head and body that the only substantive roles they can really fill are that of chauffeur and time manager.

It is easy to blame parents for not doing more to nurture the faith life of their children, but the evidence strongly suggests that congregational leadership has not equipped parents for their spiritual role, nor has the leadership even supported them in the possibilities. Parents know what is expected of them, and they feel a sense of incompetence.

Tadpole Tale: A pastor's apology

One pastor over the course of his congregational ministry realized that he had unintentionally worked against the faith formation of children and youth by not edifying and equipping parents to be active participants in the faith lives of their children. He was invited back to one of the congregations he had served to be part of festivities celebrating the congregation's fortieth anniversary. When he rose to speak to those gathered for the celebration, he included in his comments an apology. He apologized for misunderstanding his ministry in their midst and for undermining their ministry. He confessed that he had formerly thought that it was his job to raise their children for them in the Christian faith. He also noted that those efforts in isolation from strong parental participation had largely failed. He had undermined the office of parent by assuming that all they were to do was to bring their children to him. It didn't work.

This pastor's comments might have poured cold water on the celebration but, to the contrary, numerous conversations were initiated with adults who shared their own concerns and confusion as to how best to help their children, grandchildren, godchildren, and Sunday school children to grow up confident of life in the grace of God. The conversations were candid, humble, and full of mutual support and encouragement for new possibilities in the future. That night a number of Christians learned that the church's mission is only effective when it acknowledges and supports the church frog legs that give it mobility and power.

Reviewing all five recommendations in light of the importance of the partnership between home and congregations would be a valuable exercise. Families provide the basic building block for the growth and development of people's lives, including children, youth, and adults of all ages. Families are in need of a supportive community to guide them in their vital work of nurturing faith. It is not a question of whether or not parents influence children in their faith formation. Rather, the question is how that influence will take place and what messages, beliefs, and values are conveyed to children and youth.

Tadpole Tale: How is worship holy time?

To be in a meaningful and active partnership with households, congregations need to communicate and support ways that worship can be expanded beyond the public worship of the congregation (usually one hour per week). Worship happens at mealtime, bedtime, devotional time, service time, indeed, anytime. Worship is not only an experience away from daily "real life" settings, but is the center of "real life." It is real not by isolating the experience from the rest of the world, but by seeing the rest of life in the context of the means of grace, prayer, praise, and thanksgiving. Christian worship does not separate itself from moments of time, but frames these other moments in faith, hope, and love; then *all* moments are conceived and imagined in the life, death, and resurrection of Jesus. Worship shapes the lives of Christians and orders their "days and . . . deeds in [God's] peace."[2]

Kari was a college student going through a tough time as she began the second semester of her junior year. Her life was filled with meaningful, challenging work, friends, outdoor activities, and a strong passion for advocacy for peace and justice issues, yet, as the semester began, she found herself feeling down and depressed. She didn't appear to be clinically depressed, just caught in a moment unfamiliar to her. Not much seemed important to her, and not much got her excited. Although she was not an active participant in her campus ministry program, she went to see the campus pastor. They visited, but she recognized it as simply one step in a larger journey toward emotional health. Kari had a friend who was familiar with one of her favorite worship services from childhood: Holden Evening Prayer, a prayer service commissioned by Holden Village, an ecumenical Christian retreat center outside of Chelan, Washington. Her family had prayed that prayer service in her own home, and though it was a long time since she had prayed it, now seemed like the right time. Together these two college students lit candles in Kari's rented house. They sang, prayed, and read the liturgy. It connected her with her family, her God, her childhood, her lifetime of experiences in the presence of her gracious and loving God, and it was another step on a larger journey toward emotional, and spiritual, health.

We do not mean to propose that Christian worship is simply a balance between liturgical moments in the congregation and those in the home. Rather, we are suggesting that through such rituals both in public *and* domestic settings, we are helped to frame our existence in the context of the love of God and the calling to follow Jesus. If Kari's congregational worship experience were her only means of worship, she would have missed something vital to her daily life and faith. Without Kari's childhood family faith life, which included various worship experiences, she would not have been as likely to use a comforting prayer service with a friend. Kari's experience is one example of how the church is more than that which takes place in the congregation.

Croaks, Ribbits, and Hops

This book avoids using the term *church* as a synonym for the life and ministry of the local congregation. The term *church* here refers to the larger life of the people of God that includes both the congregation and the life of Christians in homes and other settings.

- In conversations, be aware of the distinction between church and the more restricted term congregation. Try to use the term congregation rather than the word church when referring to the congregation specifically. Instead of saying, "I'm going to church," try, "I'm going to my congregation," or, "I'm going to worship at my congregation." It may sound forced and difficult to do, but it will create a consciousness that "church" is more than what takes place at a certain building.

• List ways that you can imagine how the ministry of your congregation supports and strengthens your ministry in daily life in and through your home.

• List ways that you can imagine how your ministry in daily life in and through your own home supports and strengthens the ministry of your congregation.

NOTES

1. *Luther's Works, vol. 45,* The Estate of Marriage, 1522, Walther I. Brandt, ed. (Philadelphia: Fortress Press, 1962), 46.
2. *Lutheran Book of Worship* (Minneapolis: Augsburg Fortress, 1978), 163.

Principle 3—
The Legs of the Church Frog:
Home is church, too

If the church involves a living, dynamic relationship between the ministry of the congregation and the ministry of the home, then it is axiomatic that the home is church, too, where Christ is present in faith. This is the heart of the shift of thinking from the institutional, programmatic, professional understanding of church to one that operates as a living, breathing organism that imagines, gathers, scatters, and moves in the world as a distinct body in innumerable and dynamic ways.

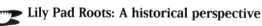 ### Lily Pad Roots: A historical perspective

This paradigm shift is really not new. It involves a return to an understanding of the significance of the home rooted in the history of the church. From the time of the early church to the nineteenth century, the family has been called the "little church."[1] In the 1960s, the Second Vatican Council of the Roman Catholic Church placed emphasis on the family by declaring it the "domestic church." Throughout the span of time and diverse Christian traditions, the role of parents and family life in the Christian nurture of children has been central. What is remarkable is how this vast consensus has succumbed to amnesia on the importance of the home in the life of the church. This amnesia has been a major factor in the recent decline of the church's ability to pass on the Christian faith to subsequent generations.

The organic, church is alive and well in the home and away from home (see Deuteronomy 6:4-9). Whether on a Sunday morning at corporate worship, Tuesday morning on the way to work, or Friday night with friends gathered together for a barbeque, the church moves, leaps, interacts with, and impacts the surrounding environment, even though no committee-sponsored programs or paid or volunteer staff have organized or led the activity. Programs and staff are not bad, but the current overdependence on them has led to a church whose legs have atrophied and are not as mobile as they once were.

Lily Pad Roots: Don't shoot the messengers

Please understand, this is not an anti-clergy or anti-congregational position. Quite the contrary, the unrealistic reliance on paid staff and volunteers to keep "the church" operating has created a church environment filled with much frustration and even bitterness. Those who are called to lead the life of the publicly gathered church are often discouraged because of the difficulty in activating the larger church body. Many "if onlys" exist in the life of the institutional church: "If only parents would take an interest"; "If only the majority of members would care enough to contribute a miniscule amount of time and finances"; "If only our worship attendance was up"; "If only our young adults would come back." Pastors, directors of youth and family ministry, Christian education directors, music directors, and other staff members and volunteers are often overwhelmed with the task before them. Their bravery and tenacity are deserving of praise, but at the same time they need to be allowed to step off the merry-go-round. It is not right, fair, or realistic to keep the church operating with such dependence on an overactive church frog head that exists at the expense of the rest of the body and at the expense of the lives and families of these faithful, passionate, often energetic-beyond-belief church workers. Recognizing that the home is church is not contrary to the work of these dedicated souls in the congregation, but necessary for their survival!

Lily Pad Roots: Don't shoot the troops, either

Nor is this principle intended as a chastisement of parents and other caregivers. Pastors and teachers are recognizing how little can be accomplished without the help of the home. Resentment has existed among church professionals concerning the inactivity of parents in the life of faith. But this is not a fair accusation of parents and guardians. After decades of implicitly telling parents and guardians that they have nothing to offer (by implying that parents and guardians are not experts and lack the skills, training, and insights to form faith), what can the professionals expect? Parents and guardians need to be esteemed, encouraged, and trained for their vital role in nurturing faith, values, and character formation. At the same time pastors and other Christian leaders in our congregations need to be relieved of unrealistic expectations of what they can accomplish without the active engagement of the home. The solution to both agendas is the same: honor and support the home as church, too.

📖 Tadpole Tale: Not here to help create a vision

Remember the old adage "If it ain't broke, don't fix it?" A parallel saying goes with it: "If it ain't workin', fix only what ain't workin'." The church is struggling to evangelize and make disciples in the western, post-industrial world, but it is not passing on the faith to its own children, let alone the unknown neighbor down the street. The church is spending much time, money, and energy trying to repair the ineffective church frog, but the parts being fixed are often the parts that are working the best! We want to fix the church frog head, yet the church's leadership receives excellent education and ongoing training, and most are faithful and good servants. We want to work on the church frog torso and in so doing, we are "preaching to the choir." We share our frustrations for a lack of attendance or commitment with the youth, the worshipers, or the choir members who show up! We rearrange worship settings and fellowship gatherings (especially youth group gatherings) as though they are the prime culprits for declining numbers.

When we, the authors, work with congregations to offer leadership training, we do not begin with the standard approach, which is to create a mission statement based on a congregationally approved vision around which both congregational leadership and membership rally. This process simply mirrors our society's indebtedness to institutional life and thinking. Congregations end up imagining what they always assume is needed: more exciting worship, more active youth groups, bigger parking lots, and perhaps more worship options from which to choose.

Rather, we come into a congregation and specifically say we are not there to help the congregation create a vision, but to offer a vision rooted in Scripture, church history, and modern research. If those who participate in this process find the presentation of the vision of a church frog with legs worth pursuing, then together we explore ways for that vision to be developed in the local congregation. (Note: We have yet to work with a congregation that has turned away from the vision of a church with head, torso, and legs.)

What we have learned is:

1. People have been thinking this way for some time, but the language and clarity of the vision has been lacking.

2. People leave saying, "I can do this. I can do this in my home and I can do this in my congregation," confident that they can live out this vision of the church.

After working with one congregation, Paul made a follow-up call to see how things were going. The pastor said, "How should I know? People are doing all kinds of things, and I can't keep track of it all." Paul asked with some alarm, "Are you concerned or bothered by what is happening?" "No, not at all," replied the pastor. "If I have to keep track of or control the work of this congregation, we will return to the ineffective ways of the past." This was a congregation that taught us much. Creative ideas, resources, and activities were emerging that neither the pastor nor we had imagined. It was the church alive and well in the home *and* the congregation.

Tadpole Tale: Let's do it again until we get it right!

David attended the annual meeting of an area Lutheran denominational judicatory.[2] The theme of the assembly was "Making Christ Known Around the World," a laudable theme that annoyed David. He wondered, "How is it that the church body can focus on evangelizing Ghana and Russia when it is not evangelizing its own homes? Our children are walking away from the church in droves and we turn our gaze overseas?" The overseas mission field is certainly important. We have much to receive as well as give in that global exchange. But it is a bit strange—dare we say hypocritical?—to spend energy on missions around the globe and not on missions for our own children. The concern is not about choosing between one or the other, but about how we can address the one so effectively and fail with the other so miserably.

Fortunately, the assembly did address local outreach as well when all the delegates and visitors were asked to turn to someone seated next to them and invite them "to church." "To church" was never defined, but it didn't have to be, for most present at the assembly assumed that "to church" meant "to weekly worship in a congregational setting." And so people complied, in their awkward, self-conscious, northern-European manner. The assembly leadership thought that if Christians practiced their invitational skills enough, they might get it right and people will feel welcomed and walk through the congregational doors and fill the pews. The institutional solution is practice: "practice makes perfect." It's the same formula that focuses evangelism on the church frog torso (corporate worship) and forgets the power of the church frog legs (the home).

In fact, many people *do* have the right tools for evangelism—to help others "come and see" Jesus—but as in the Gospel of John, the invitation is not to the Temple, the synagogue, or the latest contemporary worship service that specializes on reaching those seeking the kingdom (an admirable, but incomplete, action). The biblical invitations in John (see pages 37-38) were to more intimate settings in the manner of a sit-down, come-as-you-are dinner where people rub shoulders with others, laugh out loud, and tell stories. This setting is more likely to occur in a kitchen, dining room, or at a backyard cookout than in a congregation building. Contemporary disciples of Jesus might say, "Come and see my home where we will eat and talk, share what's important in our lives, and laugh, because the concerns and passions of our lives are too important not to laugh." Each of us can adapt these themes in words and actions natural to our own consciousness, and invite another to our home, (that is, into our lives) even if it is a camouflaged home called a restaurant, office, factory, park, school, or beach.

Responding to the synod assembly directive, David turned to the person sitting next to him at the assembly and said, "Would you like to come to my house for dinner? I would love for you to meet my family and enjoy the evening together." David then expanded on his understanding of home as church: "Once you are there, you will hear the gospel preached. It will take perhaps 20 seconds; it is called a table grace. In that moment you will hear the source of my family's hopes, dreams, comfort, and faith for this life and always. That moment may not dominate the time spent together, but then again, the Holy Spirit is not dependent on the quantity of time to start a quality relationship."

Lily Pad Roots: Surrogate families

We need to acknowledge, of course, that not every Christian child, youth, and adult lives in a home (residence) filled with other Christians. This has been true since the beginning of the church. Paul dealt with this (1 Corinthians 7:12-16), and the Gospels also address this issue. Jesus recognizes that because of him, households will be divided (see Matthew 10:34-36; Luke 12:51-53). For a person in Jesus' day, recognizing and following him as the fulfillment of the law and the prophets was to risk becoming accursed and estranged from the religious community, including one's own immediate family (see the story of the man born blind and the response of his parents in John 9:22-23). The same occurs today, especially in parts of the world dominated by other religions, such as Buddhism, Hinduism, or Islam. Sometimes opposition from a more amorphous "religion" such as consumerism or individualism can also cause domestic divisions.

The support and edification offered in this book can also be of value to homes where one or more members are not part of the Christian faith. When challenged by those who question our sensitivity to families whose members are not all confessing Christians, our response is, "What is the church doing for them now?" Most must respond, "Not much." Our assertion is that the principles and recommendations offered here can be of immeasurable support to those who feel alone in their own homes and are in need of strong and healthy church frog legs. Such legs take on the appearance of a faith bond with people outside the domestic walls and yet are not limited to congregational gatherings and programs. For those individuals we offer a surrogate faith family that is more than a community that sits together once a week and chats for a few social moments over coffee and donuts. Rather, the recommended surrogate faith family routinely communicates and prays with, serves, and develops rituals and traditions that link these people's lives in a meaningful and nurturing way.

The vast majority of American families are functional enough to support the nurture and development of their children. This means some families are struggling for survival and equilibrium in their family processes. For these families, Martin Luther's assertion seems particularly appropriate: "All who stand as masters stand in the place of parents."[3] Surrogate, adoptive, and secondary individuals and families can provide the additional support a child or youth needs in order to thrive. They can stand in the place of parents. A congregation can help develop these additional parents, providing legs to the church frog in the home.

However, even the families who are seemingly operating well need support. A myth exists in our culture that defines a healthy family as a mom and a dad raising children. We certainly approve of and celebrate this family structure. Yet, even these two-parent homes need additional support from the larger community of Christ, indeed all homes need a larger net of support to help raise children in the faith.

One of our colleagues was struggling with his teenage son. He had a friend who was having the same experience with his daughter. Ironically, the teenage son idolized the father of the teenage daughter and vice versa, so the dads got together and did a swap of sorts. They covenanted to keep a relationship going with each other's teenager. In this way, they knew that their own child would have a significant and caring "parent" in their life, even if, at the moment, the parent was not biological. One family took the daughter on a significant mission trip, and the other family involved the son in service outreach to at-risk youth. The teens had no idea, the parents were relieved, and the process of faith and character development continued.

Whether families are functioning well or struggling, the church frog torso and head can give legs to their efforts by equipping mentors and surrogate parents. Parenting classes can be offered, and times can be created in which parents can compare notes and seek mutual support. Often it is the shared wisdom of parents in the process of trying to be Christian families that is most effective in keeping those frog legs strong.

Congregations can also ask the right question. Often congregational leaders ask, "How do we get people/families involved?" This is an important question but there is one other that is more significant: "How can we help parents/grandparents/godparents become evangelists to their own children in their own homes?" This second question gets at building up the legs of the church frog.

Tadpole Tale: How to lose a friend with one visit

Another problem arises when one understands the goal of inviting another to church primarily as inviting another to the corporate worship of the congregation. The church (primarily the church frog head, but also the church frog torso) tends to overestimate the ease with which "non-churchgoers" should be able to step over the threshold of a worship space. Actually, it is more threatening than many realize, not simply because the form of worship may feel foreign, whether highly liturgical or not. Entering into a corporate worship space means entering an entire subculture of friendships, language, values, ethics, and, of course, religious creed(s). The insider recognizes that all is not uniform; people speak to some and ignore others, worship styles and preferences vary, the values, ethics, and Christian theologies present are diverse and not always in agreement. But to the outsider, it all looks like a monolithic temple of God (or perhaps a tower of Babel!)

Jonathan, a 16-year-old youth, routinely joined his parents in worship on Sunday morning. He was bored by the experience, but instead of challenging his parents wishes for him to attend worship services, he decided to ask his friend to join him. His thinking was, "It is best not to be bored alone." Jonathan did not have many friends, so he was inviting his one and only identifiable friend. But, the friend and the friend's family were offended. They interpreted the invitation as a judgment on the family for their lack of faith and moral character. The friend turned away from Jonathan and would not associate with him anymore. Jonathan's invitation to join him "at church" cost him dearly.

Tadpole Tale: Hindus live here

While working with the church in Guyana, South America, we attended the Hindu funeral of a good friend. Upon entering the home of this Hindu family, we noticed a shrine or altar in one corner of the room. Included were pictures of Hindu gods, smoking incense, plants, and herbs. It was the place for the family to worship in their home. We later learned that every Hindu home has such an altar arrangement. Walk into a home and it says, "Hindus live here!"

At the same funeral we listened to the leader critically comment on the changing culture of Hindu Guyanese. The Hindu leader was concerned about losing the young people to the seductions of materialism and individualism. Any Christian pastor would have been proud to give the same sermon. Hindus as well as Christians are concerned about connecting and passing on their faith to the next generation. The Hindus in Guyana have an advantage, however. They have altars in their homes.

Where is the place in our homes that says, "Christians live here?" Where is the Christian altar in our homes? It may be located in many places such as the dinner table around which Christians commune and share. Perhaps it is the room in which the family congregates and talks. Most likely this place does not have a screen. In the Christian parenting video series *It Takes More than Love*, Thelma Buchner and her many children and foster children identify the piano in their home as the place where love, values, and faith were passed on.[4] This was their Christian altar. Sadly, many Christian families do not eat together any longer, so the Christian altar of the dinner table is often neglected; and also, sadly, many families no longer gather intentionally for conversation, so this sacred place goes unused. And do any families gather around a piano anymore?

Whether it is the dinner table, the living room, or the piano, the point is that the home needs to be church, too. A home altar may not be the last word in developing the home as church, but it is an important component. To see a sign, a reminder of God's presence and a lifestyle devoted to God, reveals a lot about a home. The addition of a home altar as part of the consciousness of the home promotes the home as a place where the faith is practiced. We know that the television or computer is not a home altar. One of our former students put it this way: "If you have more screens in your home than you have meals together in a week, then you have problems!" We heartily agree.

Lily Pad Roots: An old question revisited

The question of whether current generations will be able to pass on their Christian faith to future generations is an ancient one, and appears to be a central concern to which the writer of Deuteronomy repeatedly returns. What will happen to the children, and the children's children? Will they know the stories of faith, the stories of the scriptures, the stories of the covenant family?

After the destruction of Jerusalem and Judah in 587 B.C.E., the Hebrew people had deep concerns about their future as a unique people, that is, as people who followed the God of Abraham, Isaac, and Jacob (Deuteronomy 30:20). While in captivity in Babylon, the people, inspired in part by the prophetic encouragement of individuals like Jeremiah and Ezekiel, developed a fourfold response to ensure that faith in the God of their ancestors would not be lost. Synagogue worship was established in the absence of the destroyed temple in Jerusalem. A rabbinical order emerged, and the sacred texts were gathered and edited to aid in the teaching of the faith to subsequent generations. And, perhaps the most critical measure of all: the faith of the people was incorporated into the life of the home. The rituals, the storytelling, the scripted didactic conversations and home liturgies, the prayers, and the Scriptures were all made a part of the life of the home.[5]

The strategic move of focusing on the home and the role of parents, grandparents, and others who care for children is evident in Deuteronomy. A central theme in Deuteronomy is that the adult generations not forget the great deeds of the God who brought them out of bondage and into freedom, and to keep God's commandments, statutes, and ordinances. Moses says to the people, "But take care and watch yourselves closely, so as neither to forget the things that your eyes have seen nor to let them slip from your mind all the days of your life; make them known to your children and your children's children—how you once stood before the LORD your God at Horeb, when the LORD said to me, 'Assemble the people for me, and I will let them hear my words, so that they may learn to fear me as long as they live on the earth, and may teach their children so . . .'" (Deuteronomy 4:10).

Redundancy of message is the teaching approach in Deuteronomy. These key themes are stated and restated so that the people will remember their charge to tell the story of God's care for the people, a heavenly care that included a unique way of life expressed in the covenant language of commandments, statutes, and ordinances. Not only is the teaching made clear through repetition in the text, but the people themselves are to repeat it again and again. Deuteronomy presents a formula for covenant renewal. The covenant God made with the people at Horeb (Sinai) is to be embraced by each new generation. When Moses says to the people, "And what other great nation has statutes and ordinances as just as this entire law that I am setting before you today?" (Deuteronomy 4:8), the word *today* is more than a reference to a sermon given long ago by Moses. The word *today* is meant to enlist each generation in the act of covenant renewal. The word *today* implies the sense of here and now for every generation of the people of God. If the words are read or heard on October 21, 2003, then the word *today* means October 21, 2003 (see Deuteronomy 5:3; 6:6; 7:11; 11:2, 8, 26, 28; 26:17-18; 28:1, 15; 29:13-15; 30:11, 15).

Deuteronomy 6:4-9 contains the Shemah: "Hear, O Israel: The LORD is our God, the LORD alone" (Deuteronomy 6:4). This is the most important and unique confessional state-ment of the people of Israel, and is recited two times daily by faithful Jews to this day. In this famous passage the people were told to recite the message revealed by Moses "to your children and talk about them when you are at home and when you are away, when you lie down and when you rise" (6:7). God's people were to recite and have con-versation regarding the teachings and the commandments, and to do it everywhere and at all times. The people were to remember these words of life and faith through the visi-ble presence of the word of God that was to be written and placed on their bodies, doorposts, and gates (6:8-9).

Here the centerpiece of the classroom for faith transmission is the home. The home is the place where people dwell, from which they go out and to which they return at the close of the day. The lessons are found in daily life experiences and the instructors are the immediate caregivers with whom children are in contact day in and day out. As chil-dren and adults leave and return to their dwellings, they are reminded of the teachings of the faith that are inscribed on doors and gates. They are encouraged to talk about the word of God even through such concrete reminders as having the written words affixed to their very persons.

In language reminiscent of the Shemah, Proverbs 6:20-22 explains the impact of the message of the faith taught in the home. The text begins, "My child, keep your father's commandment, and do not forsake your mother's teaching. Bind them upon your heart always; tie them around your neck" (Proverbs 6:20-21). The benefit of this obedience is described in terms of guidance, protection, and a consciousness of what is true and valuable: "When you walk, they will lead you; when you lie down, they will watch over you; and when you awake, they will talk with you" (Proverbs 6:22). The commandments and teachings of the parents will make a significant difference in the life of the child but, obviously, only if the parents teach and the child listens. When both happen, the message of the faith is communicated. The words of faith guide, protect, and engage the child in the child's mind. It becomes a part of the child; it shapes who the child is.

Tadpole Tale: Shaping a child's life

Children are beautiful, open, receptive, malleable creatures, highly influenced by their caregivers. Eric had two loving grandparents who adored him. He knew that he was the apple of their eyes. They expressed that in their warm and loving words and in their conduct, care, and interest in his life. In their grandparenting, they taught Eric how to grow up safely, wisely, and faithfully. They read to him, played with him, prayed with him, watched over him, and taught him things he could master (like walking, talking, playing games, and singing with the angels). They showed him what he could do and what was not safe or good to do.

Eric's parents would take him and his little sister to his grandparents' house. Needing to be the first person through the front door, he would burst into the house yelling with exuberance, "Hello everybody, I'm here." Eric knew he was of supreme value. When he entered the home, the world he knew was ready to stop and take note, "Hello everybody, I'm here." He felt safe and loved, a protective care hovered over him, and one can imagine the internal conversations he had, recalling the words communicated to him from two loving grandparents. Like the loving ministry of these two grandparents, the Christian faith is to be embedded in the lives of our children. This happens with words, sights, sounds, hugs, winks, and a general demeanor and conduct that guide, protect, and speak to children in ways that remind them of the power of the faith for their every breath, every heartbeat, and every step.

Lily Pad Roots: The domestic nature of the church as springboard to the world

Earlier, we spoke of the connection between the domestic church and the public church as demonstrated in the books of Acts. What is also evident in that book is that the domestic church is the springboard for evangelism into the world. The church expanded to the Gentiles through the household of Cornelius, a Roman military commander. When Peter visited Cornelius, he spoke not only to Cornelius but also to "his relatives and close friends" (Acts 10:24). Cornelius, together with the others gathered for the occasion, heard the word of God from Peter, received the Holy Spirit, and was baptized that very day (10:44-48). Through the ministry of the home, the church, composed of both Jewish and non-Jewish (Gentile) believers, began that day. The account of that event ends with the words, "Then they invited him to stay for several days" (10:48). Cornelius and the others who gathered to hear and receive God's word and be baptized asked Peter to remain and continue to nurture them in faith. Most likely they "devoted themselves to the apostle's teaching and fellowship, to the breaking of bread and the prayers" (2:42).

The pattern of establishing a community of faith within households is repeated elsewhere in Acts. Lydia, a dealer in cloth from Thyatira, was baptized along with her entire household (16:14-15). Later, Paul and Silas spoke the word of God to the Philippian jailer "and to all who were in his house" (16:32), and "he and his entire family were baptized without delay" (16:33). And in Corinth, Crispus, "together with all his household" (18:8), became a believer. The repeated pattern of Acts—missionaries entering homes to evangelize—helped shape and develop the church, both in faith and numbers.

As the church expanded more deeply into the Roman Empire, it made particular inroads in the larger cities where many people did not live in private houses. People rather tended to live in *insulas*, facilities that were a combination of apartment complex and marketplace.[6] In the *insula* people had their workshops and their marketplace shops; it is where they ate, slept, worked, conversed, and bantered about contemporary views of philosophy and religion. Evangelism took place in the context of daily conversations through an established social network of family relations, friendships, and professional ties that connected missionaries with many other potential followers.[7] Likely in this environment, Paul and other missionaries carried on their most effective ministry (see 1 Thessalonians 2:9-12). Here Paul practiced his trade of leatherwork and shared the message of Jesus Christ with others (see Acts 18:1-4; Romans 16:3-5).

Although Paul began his missionary work with a focus on the public expression of faith in synagogues, his more effective ministry appears to have been in and through the homes of believers (see Acts 18:6-8; 20:20; Romans 16:5; Philippians 4:22; 2 Timothy 4:19).

Tadpole Tale: From Monday to Sunday

Two families were in the habit of taking time when they were together to reflect upon issues in life that were important to them and would often embrace the moment with faith talk, scripture readings, and prayer. This foundation developed into a relationship that both families treasured. Even as the children grew and moved away, the parents continued the pattern and found comfort as they prayed for their children and shared parental joys and concerns.

One Monday evening, the children were far from home but near to their hearts. The parents were experiencing a new found level of peace and tranquility with their children's maturation after years of struggle, the kind with which most families are familiar. The following Sunday, early in the morning, one of the mothers called the other couple imploring their prayers for a son who was in intensive care, his life in the balance with an overwhelming infection. The son died later that morning and the two families spent the day together comforting one another and planning for the days ahead. The bonds that had been there for years between the families carried them through this crisis and sustained them for years to come.

Lily Pad Roots: Marriage and family—Luther and the Reformation

Historian Steven Ozment observes that sixteenth-century church reformers were the first to categorically honor marriage above the celibate life. Others had defended family life or noted the difficulties of celibacy, but it was the reformers who emphasized marriage and family life as the preferred way to live the Christian life.[8] For centuries, the common assumption was that the best way to live the religious life was to enter the cloister. The monastery had been the premier school for faith and character, but the reformers argued that family life, not the monastic experience, was the primary arena for nurturing faith, values, and character. As Martin Luther said, "For God has exalted this walk of life above all others; indeed, he has set it up in his place on earth."[9]

PARENTS AS "APOSTLES, BISHOPS, AND PRIESTS"

Luther's zeal for supporting family life was matched by his anger at what he often observed. Upon returning from Saxony where he visited congregations and homes, he grumbled,

> Dear God, what misery I beheld! The ordinary person, especially in the villages, knows absolutely nothing about the Christian faith . . . As a result they live like simple cattle or irrational pigs and, despite the fact that the gospel has returned, have mastered the fine art of misusing all their freedom.[10]

Luther's shock and grumbling led him to write the Small Catechism, which was designed as a teaching tool to be used by parents in the home. The Small Catechism is Luther's recognition that the church frog needed legs if it was to be healthy and faith formative. Certainly some of Luther's most prophetic words, for his time and ours, were spoken as he reflected upon the need for faithful homes. He states, "Everybody acts as if God gave us children for our pleasure and amusement . . . We must not think only of amassing money and property for them."[11] These words are applicable for much of family life in America today as well. Luther had a much larger vision of the importance of parents in the life of faith. He said, "Most certainly father and mother are apostles, bishops, and priests to their children, for it is they who make them acquainted with the gospel."[12] Luther lived this conviction in his own family life. Luther believed—and acted upon his belief—that the home was foundational to passing on the faith to the next generation.

Luther and other reformers did not, however, gain this pastoral perspective in a vacuum. Catholic homes for centuries had been giving support and pastoral directives to nurture the Christian faith in the home. This occurred as part of the confessional life of the church. When adults came to the priest to offer their confession and receive absolution, part of their penance was to rededicate their lives to the Christian faith through various expressions of piety, including prayer and study. Since nearly all the peasant populace was illiterate, "studying" the faith meant hearing the message of the Bible in the hymnody and liturgy of the church, and learning the stories of the Bible through visual arts such as stained glass windows, church facades, sculpture, and paintings. Parents, guardians, and other caregivers, for example, in order to teach the message and the life of the Christian faith to children, often used woodcut prints of scenes from the life of Jesus, the Lord's Prayer or the Ten Commandments. It's likely Luther's parents and those of the other reformers used this method as part of their child rearing.

A consensus emerged during the sixteenth century as an institutional alliance between the home, congregation, and school developed. The faith was to be heard, discussed, learned, and believed in each of these settings, and the home was without question an integral part of the church's educational design. Luther promoted door and wall placards for the home that contained catechetical instruction for parents to teach their children and, consequently, for the family to study and learn together. Not only was parental involvement encouraged to help instruct children in the Christian faith, but parents were specifically held accountable for their children's catechetical instruction.

Lily Pad Roots: Faith and the home—the modern research

Recent research supports the role of the home and daily life experience in Christian faith. A notable study on the effectiveness of Christian education from the Search Institute concludes "that life experiences are strongly associated with maturity of faith. Having family and friends are two near-universal experiences that have impact on one's growth in faith maturity."[13] Further, as we observed earlier,[14] published data from the same research indicates that mothers and fathers were the top two primary faith influences in the lives of youth between the seventh and twelfth grades.

The Search Institute's research evaluated what makes for effective Christian education in congregations. Perhaps the most stunning and eye-opening conclusion was that the most important factor for faith formation did not take place in the congregation at all, but in the home. The study concluded that of the two strongest connections to faith maturity—family religiousness and lifelong Christian education—family religiousness is slightly more important. The family experiences most tied to greater faith maturity are the frequency with which an adolescent talked with his/her mother and father about faith, the frequency of family devotions, and the frequency with which parents and children together were involved in efforts, formal or informal, to help other people. Each of these family experiences is more powerful than the frequency with which an adolescent sees his or her parents engage in religious behavior like church attendance.[15]

Congregations that are concerned about maturing faith and reaching out to others with the Christian faith, therefore, recognize the influence of homes as essential. Whether in the biblical witness, church history, or modern research, the evidence is overwhelming that the home is a primary sphere of influence for faith formation. The family is recognized as the "little church" or the "domestic church." Parents are "apostles, bishops, and priests," and the home is a primary arena for Christian education, discipleship, and evangelism.

Lily Pad Roots: Home as metaphor for a larger sphere of influence

Earlier in the chapter we introduced a clarification and expansion of the term "home." As the term "family" is intended as an inclusive term, so "home" is intended to represent a larger sphere of life beyond our daily dwellings. We are to be "at home" in the world because it is a world that God loves—a place in which we are never apart from God's presence and redeeming love. We can be "at home" with friends, with family on vacation, at work, at a gathering in our congregation, and "at home" in our livingrooms. After the terrorist attacks on the World Trade Center and the Pentagon in 2001, an increased sense of a national identity and a national "home" emerged. A national news commentator, speaking on the evening of September 11th, observed that a sense of "family" embraced the country. This is natural language. When a bond is made through personal relationships, a championship team, or a national disaster, a sense of unity develops, creating an awareness of the need to foster—and even celebrate—a common good; to "rejoice with those who rejoice, weep with those who weep" (Romans 12:15).

Croaks, Ribbits, and Hops

If the home is church, too, then the home needs to be guided by and operate under that premise.

- An exercise that can help in this process is for people who live together and people who commune together in some other way to develop a mission statement for their life together. Here is an example of a mission statement for the home: "The _____ family are children of God living lives of *thanksgiving* by valuing: education, each other, God's creation, laughter, food, health, friends, plants, life, air, music, shelter, the community of Christians, self-worth, stability, service to others, creativity, and respecting others. Grateful for our past; working to pass on a good future." Working together as a family unit, write a mission statement for your life together.

- Working with family or friends, identify and create a setting for your own home altar. Perhaps it could be located in special corner of a room, or in a place outdoors, or in a common gathering spot that has special meaning for you and others. Your home altar could include a water fountain, chirping birds, soft lights or candles, a Bible, a cross, or a faith image. Colorful fabrics and other decorations can add to the mood and theme of a church season, or one of the seasons of nature. Freshly baked bread or some other appealing aroma can add to a worshipful setting. Wherever that place, set it apart with prayer, color, conversation, and a sense that it is a place to rest together, to be nurtured, cared for, and to grow together. Let it be a place where you "let the word of Christ dwell in you richly" (Colossians 3:16). The space itself is not holy ground. It is holy ground because holy time has been shared there.

- Review how you as an individual and as a household or friendship community welcome people to your home and into your lives. How do you practice what the apostle Paul exhorts in Romans 15:7: "Welcome one another, therefore, just as Christ has welcomed you, for the glory of God"? Do you extend a hand of friendship or offer a hug? Do you take coats or other items that are awkward to keep by one's side? How quickly are you ready to offer something to drink or eat? Do you tend to the comfort of your guests? Do you turn off the television or turn down loud music? Explore ways that you would want to be welcomed, and experiment with these ideas by trying them out with family, friends, and even strangers.

• Schedule weekly family meetings (see pages 131-132 in chapter 9).

NOTES

1. *The Child in Christian Thought,* Marcia Bunge, ed. (Grand Rapids: Eerdmans Publishing Co., 2001), 21.
2. Synod assembly; a "synod" is a grouping of congregations in a geographical region for mission and ministry.
3. See note, page 25 (Kolb/Wengert, 406).
4. *It Takes More than Love* (Minneapolis: Seraphim Communications, Lutheran Social Services, Fairview Behavioral Services, 1995).
5. Loren B. Mead, *Five Challenges for the once and Future Church* (New York: The Alban Institute, 1996), 84.
6. Abraham J. Halherbe, *Paul and the Thessalonians* (Philadelphia: Fortress Press, 1987), 17.
7. Ibid., 17-19.
8. Steven Ozment, *When Father's Ruled: Family Life in Reformation Europe* (Cambridge: Harvard University Press, 1983), 7.
9. *The Book of Concord: The Confessions of the Evangelical Lutheran Church,* Robert Kolb and Timothy J. Wengert, eds. (Minneapolis: Fortress Press, 2000), 403-404.
10. Ibid., 347-348.
11. Ibid., 409-410.
12. *Luther's Works,* vol. 45, The Estate of Marriage, 1522, Walther I. Brandt, ed. (Philadelphia: Fortress Press, 1962), 46.
13. Peter L. Benson and Carolyn H. Eklin, *Effective Christian Education: A National Study of Protestant Congregations, A Report for the Evangelical Lutheran Church in America* (Minneapolis: Search Institute, 1990), 49.
14. See page 28.
15. Peter L. Benson and Carolyn H. Eklin, *Effective Christian Education: A Summary Report on Faith, Loyalty, and Congregational Life* (Minneapolis: Search Institute, 1990), 38.

CHAPTER Six

Principle 4—The Sticky Frog Tongue: Faith is caught more than taught

Just as a frog catches its prey with a long, sticky tongue, so faith is caught more than taught. This fourth theme, popularized by John Westerhoff, has been around for years, but when it is shared with those who have a passion for education, it is often resisted. A religion professor at a Christian college wondered how one could support such a notion at an institution dedicated to formal learning. Once it was explained that the principle advocates learning in addition to and beyond the classroom, not as a substitute for it, the professor was somewhat relieved. This principle does not attack formal education, but does insist that much human learning is experiential. Similarly, the formation of a living and vital faith also cannot be restricted to formal learning experiences such as Sunday school or a confirmation class.

Good academic learning does not restrict the tools and procedures of learning to books and the gathering of theories and data. Even in academic life, what is learned is caught and not merely taught. Experiential learning, service learning, and personal observations and impressions can be incorporated into meaningful classroom education. Today learners and teachers are increasingly encouraged to acquire valuable insights and data from daily life encounters, and to attach valuable insights to these encounters. One of the great challenges of education is to connect information and life experiences. Without this connection, the learning does not make sense in people's lives, and is valuable only as a need to pass a test.

Lily Pad Roots: Teaching outside the walls

The principle that faith is caught more than taught simply reminds pastors, Christian educators, godparents, grandparents, and parents that Jesus often taught his followers in a classroom without walls. His message was received along roads that led in and out of Galilee, Samaria, and Judea. Yet, though Jesus gave insightful information about the kingdom of God, and spoke of his saving work, his disciples often did not get it. The disciples were chastised for their "little faith" (see Matthew 6:30; 8:26; 14:31; 16:08; 17:20) and their hard hearts (Mark 6:52; see Mark 8:17). At times his followers received divine revelation that would only later be understood (see Matthew 17:9; Luke 24:6-9; John 12:16).

Lily Pad Roots: Peter, the rock who caught the faith

Perhaps the best biblical example of faith that is caught is Peter. Historically, Peter has been thought of as the source of teaching authority in the church (though the church is divided as to what exactly this role means). Beyond the questions of ecclesiology and church politics is the question of how it is that Peter serves as a source of teaching authority. A pivotal answer is in this principle (especially as it is addressed in Matthew).

The gospel writer Matthew understands Peter to be a leading and representative disciple (see Matthew 10:2; 14: 28-31; 16:13-20; 17:24-27). In Matthew 16:16-19, Peter alone makes a confession of faith, "You are the Christ, the Son of the living God." Only in Matthew does Jesus reward this bold act of faith with the words, "And I tell you, you are Peter, and on this rock I will build my church." Peter is identified in Matthew with the authoritative teaching of Jesus, with the faithful confession of the church, with the failures and joys of being a follower of Jesus, and as one whose character is central to the development of the early church.

Peter is confessor and leader, but most essentially Peter is the model teacher of the Christian faith in that he himself experiences the power of forgiveness and new life. The text that illumines this most clearly is Matthew 10:26-33. In this text, Jesus exhorts the disciples to bold proclamation even in the midst of persecution and great peril—the kind of boldness that risks stepping out onto a stormy sea and expects to walk on water (Matthew 14:28-31). But verse 33 is the thorn for Peter, ". . . but whoever denies me before others, I also will deny before my Father in heaven." The key word is *deny*. In the Matthew account of Peter's denial of Jesus (26:69-75), Peter not only denied that he was with Jesus, he did so "before all of them" (verse 70). The text concludes in

Matthew, Mark, and Luke with Peter leaving and weeping bitterly, but only in Matthew is this story the last mention of Peter, the rock of the church, in the Gospel!

Of the four Gospels, only Matthew has no post-resurrection accounts that include Peter by name. So we are drawn back to the body of Matthew to recall that Peter was designated the leader, the confessor, and the teacher of the earliest church. By the end of the Gospel of Matthew, it becomes clear that Peter could well be that representative voice of the message of the gospel, for he himself, as the church knew well, experienced the full extent of that message. Peter was not only taught the message of forgiveness and new life from Jesus, he caught and experienced the full intent of Jesus' message and work of salvation for sinful, needy humanity.

Tadpole Tale: Gotcha!

Not only Peter and the early church, but also children and youth learn valuable lessons from what they experience, see, and hear around them. They are learning from others around them all the time, especially parents, and often they learn through the mistakes of adults.

Many parents have had the "gotcha" experience with their teenager. Paul and his family have developed an important tradition: they enjoy vacationing on a Wisconsin lake every summer. Primary activities for the vacation include lathering up with suntan lotion, taking their boat out to an isolated spot on the lake, dropping anchor, laying back in the boat seats, and reading their favorite novels in the hot sun. Eventually, when they get too warm, the family leaps off the boat into the deep cool waters of the lake where they float and swim and cool down. They then crawl back into the boat, lather up again, scarf down some snack food and a soft drink, and return to their novels. The cycle is repeated all day long.

The Hill family boat is of special significance to Paul. Having spent every summer of his youth on a northern Minnesota lake, Paul takes great pride in the maintenance of the boat and his boating knowledge and skills. In fact, in the family, the boat is called "Dad's poopsy," a term of endearment applied only to the most important of material objects. It is common knowledge never to mess with "Dad's poopsy." The children have been meticulously schooled in how to maintain the boat and drive it. Flexibility and innovation are not encouraged, for it is expected that they will do it the way *dad* does it.

On one warm, sunny, summer day, the Hill family was engaged in its "lather, read, swim, eat, and repeat" ritual. When it was time to head back to the cabin, Paul started the motor and pushed the throttle forward. The engine groaned and died. He started it again, and again it groaned and died. It was acting as if something was holding it back. Paul checked for weeds around the propeller. It was clear. On the third attempt he shoved the throttle forward hard. The boat seemed stuck and then suddenly it lurched forward. At the same time a loud bang was heard as the anchor hit the side of the boat.

The two Hill teenagers at first were stunned and then, upon realizing dad had actually tried to take off while the anchor was still down, began to laugh uncontrollably. Humiliation is not worn well on the perfect captain. This is a "gotcha."

Lily Pad Roots: We are the curriculum

Our youth and children are watching and learning from us all the time. When they learn in adolescence that we are not perfect humans, they are amused and can even glory in watching us fail, flounder, and stumble. What we do, all that we do, teaches. The classroom is always open and we are always on display, so what we do matters.

ACTIONS DO SPEAK LOUDER THAN WORDS

Educators use a common phrase, "We are the curriculum," which can be applied far beyond the classroom. Children, youth, adults, parents, grandparents, relatives, friends, co-workers, classmates, and many others make up the daily learning laboratory. The church is always a teaching church. As educators for faith and life, it is worthless to tell our children "do as I say, and not as I do." They will watch our actions first, and our actions carry the most weight. Parents are especially aware of this with teenagers. They listen to parents and other authority figures in their lives with their eyes more than their ears.

God literally has "hardwired" our brains to learn in this fashion. Experiments with new-born infants demonstrate that the human brain is specifically designed to seek out the face of another human. When babies less than 24 hours old are shown four pictures: a face, a scrambled face, an unsymmetrical face, and a blank card, the infants most likely will follow the normal face.[1] Researchers note that "a face-like pattern elicits a greater extent of tracking behavior than does a non-face-like pattern."[2] Our brains are created in this way. Researchers note that we are even born with specific brain cells whose task is to find the face or the hand of another human being. Unlike most of our brain cells, which do not initially selectively differentiate, these cells do. For example, evidence shows that no "selective visual responses in babies to such objects as fruit, tree branches, and other objects" exist. "Only the face and hands provide evidence of selective cell ensemble activity."[3] In other words, we are created to be in relationships. We are created to track other humans, to watch them, to engage them and to learn from them. It is the way we are made.

Parents delight in this innate ability of babies. We'll stare into the face of babies and make faces, coo, and smile. The baby then mirrors this behavior for us. As we animate our faces so do they. Not surprisingly, the human face has "44 separate facial muscles, four involve chewing and 40 involve facial expression. No other species has such capacity for making faces!"[4] This is the earliest form of communication we have with our children, and comes at the beginning of their faith formation.

To be made in the image of God is to be made to track others. Humans seek out the face to watch and listen for the voice to hear. It is good news when John says, "the Word (voice) became flesh (face) and lived among us" (John 1:14; see also 10:1-4). Our brain structure reveals God in a way that our brains can track, in the words and face of Jesus Christ.

The principle "faith is caught more than taught" reflects this foundational insight about humans and our brains. When teenagers give us a "gotcha" it is a reminder to us that they were born watching us and they never stop. They are always reading, evaluating, and critiquing us and other adults around them. If they sense that adults are insincere, phony, or contrived, they will note it and check them off their credible list. On the other hand, if they sense sincerity, love, commitment, and faith, then they will learn to be sincere, to love, to make commitments, and to claim their faith.

Tadpole Tale: The truth-telling fourth grader

A fourth grader made this point perfectly clear. One hot, Texas summer afternoon, an adult was supervising a large group game on an open field. One hundred twenty kids were playing "capture the flag." The heat was a concern. Running in mid-afternoon Texas heat can be dangerous. The supervisor was watching closely to make sure that no one was getting too over-heated. As his eyes surveyed the field looking for signs of distress, a young girl stood in front of him and talked with great animation. The supervisor was listening to her with one ear, but his eyes continually moved away from her to the field. Suddenly, he heard the nasal voice of her fourth-grade friend saying, with righteous indignation, "You're not really listening to her!" The supervisor looked at her and said, "How do you know that?" She responded, "Because you are not looking at her." Gotcha!! Faith is caught more than taught, and even on the sidelines of a large Texas field, this adult was at the front of the classroom.

Lilly Pad Roots: Keep your eyes on Jesus

The church is always teaching—through individual and collective actions, gestures, words, and policies as well as inactivity, silence, and distant stares. The question is, "In each local setting of the church, whether the public, institutional, or home church, what is being taught?" Is the church teaching care and attention, or inattentiveness with a distant stare?

Jesus makes it clear that the pivotal factor in being a disciple is singular attention to and relationship with him. Only through Jesus can the disciples focus on others and the needs of the world. All clear vision in the church begins with seeing Jesus. Disciples are to look at him, look into his face, a face that is now revealed through the eyes, ears, hands, and feet of others, that is, the body of Christ. Those others include uncles and aunts, grandparents, parents, as well as pastors and Sunday school teachers.

Of course, we keep our eyes on Jesus as one who teaches. He teaches his own twelve and others who followed him for three years, as well as all subsequent generations of disciples. And yet, even Jesus' teaching is caught and not just taught with words of divine wisdom. The Gospel of Mark identifies occasions when Jesus taught the people, but we, the readers, never learn specifically what was taught (see Mark 1:21-28; 2:2, 13). Further, instead of understanding his teachings, Jesus' disciples are reprimanded for their hardness of heart (6:52, 8:17). Peter makes a confession of faith and seems to understand, but Jesus must rebuke him for rejecting what must be: Jesus' death and resurrection. Even after the resurrection, Jesus' own followers don't get it. The women run away and say nothing to anyone out of fear (16:8). In Luke the disciples treat the women's account of seeing the resurrected Jesus as an old wives' tale (Luke 24:11). Thomas has to see for himself in John (John 20:25). In Matthew, members of Jesus' inner group of followers see the resurrected Lord but still doubt (Matthew 28:17). Yet, Jesus sends them out with the Great Commission anyway. The good news for followers of all time is that Jesus does not send the doubters away but sends them out to make other disciples (28:19-20). Apparently, Jesus is confident that on the road, in the midst of the word of God and daily life experience, they would, by the grace of God, understand the message of the gospel in ways they never grasped in words alone.

The challenge of discipleship is to hear and see Jesus. Jesus says, "No one can serve two masters; for a slave will either hate the one and love the other, or be devoted to the one and despise the other. You cannot serve God and wealth" (Matthew 6:24). Using hyperbole, Jesus goes so far as to assert, "Whoever comes to me and does not hate father and mother, wife and children, brothers and sisters, yes, and even life itself, cannot be my disciple" (Luke 14:26). Matthew clarifies the intent of Jesus' words: "Whoever loves father or mother more than me is not worthy of me; and whoever loves son or daughter more than me is not worthy of me; and whoever does not take up the cross and follow me is not worthy of me" (Matthew 10:37). Only through a relationship with Jesus, through whom God reconciled the world, can one establish a reconciling relationship with the world. Jesus gives us core beliefs and values as the foundation for how one lives. To pay attention to the world is first and foremost to pay attention to Jesus.

Lilly Pad Roots: Hypocrisy versus integrity

The implication of this perspective is that the common American separation of personal or private behavior from public behavior is called seriously into question. In terms of faith, we cannot live in two different and separate worlds. The nature of our ethics, the manner of our behavior, and the confession of our hearts need to be consistent both in private and public life. Nothing destroys credibility faster than hypocrisy. Nothing shakes faith more than when those whom we admire fall glaringly short of their own faith and principled life. This is not a call for adults and parents to live perfect lives, but this is a call for parents and adults to strive for consistency in their private and public lives, especially in matters of faith. Striving to see Jesus in all we say, do, and imagine is the formula and foundation for Christian consistency.

Our children are watching and learning from us every day. All Christian adults are youth ministers, whether we want to be or not. The choice is to decide whether we are going to be good at this work or not. This is why it is so important that parents and guardians do more than drop their children off at Sunday school, for example. By driving away, they say, "This is not important to me." By walking in with the children, they are saying, "This matters to me, too!" Pastors and other church leaders who say, "I don't do youth ministry," or, "I don't work well with kids," are assuming this is an option for them. It is not. They are teaching and sending a powerful message to youth and children by ignoring them. Our experience is that church leaders and pastors, including the senior pastor, who make a commitment to giving time and energy to youth and their families are likely to have healthy, thriving congregations.

In addition, pastors and other congregational leaders dare not ignore their own families and their own children, for they are members of the church as well—the church in the home. One of the sad tragedies of church life, and one of growing concern, is when those in leadership crash and burn in their own families. Our conviction is that one reason for this has to do with an errant view of the church frog. Trying to fix the church frog head and the church frog torso without attention to the church frog legs just doesn't work. Not only does it frustrate congregational leadership, it also takes its toll in the homes of those same congregational leaders.

Tadpole Tale: Hope springs eternal, even when we blow it

A highly admired church camp director could rightly take credit for having mentored an entire generation of young church leaders. Summer after summer, young men and women worked at the camp he directed and were profoundly influenced by his ministry, conviction, and leadership. It seemed he was single-handedly providing seminaries with new students because of his influence. Many years later, this group of now middle-aged church leaders was shocked to learn that their mentor and hero had been arrested for sexual impropriety with minors, behavior that had been going on for more than 20 years. He was sent to prison for his actions. Naturally, these church leaders were devastated. In the days following the revelations, one spoke the heart of all when she raised the question, "Does this mean that everything we are committed to is a lie?" Their confidence was shaken to the core, but slowly, after much conversation, these leaders regained their balance, renewed their commitment, and ironically, grew to embrace a much deeper understanding of sin and grace. These people were let down. They had caught the faith from this leader and his actions as their camp director inspired and motivated them. In fact, it is a testimony to the power of the gospel that rather than reject this faith they clung to it more dearly in this time of doubt and crisis. They had indeed caught the faith to the point that it could not be jarred loose, even when the vessel of the faith broke.

Grace abounds in this story for those of us who know our feet are made of clay. Try as we may, we are not perfect. The apostle Paul captured our dilemma when he said,

> I do not understand my own actions. For I do not do what I want, but I do the very thing I hate . . . I can will what is right, but I cannot do it. For I do not do the good I want, but the evil I do not want is what I do. Now if I do what I do not want, it is no longer I that do it, but sin that dwells within me . . . Wretched man that I am! Who will rescue me from this body of death? Thanks be to God through Jesus Christ our Lord! (Romans 7:15-25).

Ultimately, even as we strive to be good adult models, we will fail. At these moments we are reminded that God is faithful still.

Lily Pad Roots: Walking the talk

Living by the principle, "Faith is caught more than taught," is not a demand for perfect living, but a call to strive for the kingdom of God (Matthew 6:33). This is the message of Jesus in the Sermon on the Mount. The issue in the Gospel of Matthew is integrity versus hypocrisy. Jesus challenges the people to understand the nature of integrity and what it means for daily life. He is very critical of those who are hypocritical, whose lives are not internally and externally consistent. A good translation of the word *hypocrisy* is "two-faced." The scribes and Pharisees were two-faced. They did not walk the talk. Their hips and their lips were sending out two different messages.

In the Sermon on the Mount, Jesus seems to make an impossible demand: "For I tell you unless your righteousness exceeds that of the scribes and Pharisees you will never enter the kingdom of heaven" (Matthew 5:20). What does Jesus mean by righteousness? Is he talking about perfect behavior? Certainly Jesus expects God's people to behave in exemplary ways, but it goes deeper than that. Righteousness refers not only to one's behavior, but also to one's heart, attitudes, and faith. As the Sermon on the Mount unfolds, Jesus gives example after example of the importance of heart and hand, or attitude and action working in harmony. It's not enough to avoid killing, we must resolve our anger with our neighbor (see 5:21-26). It's not enough for men to divorce in legally prescribed ways, they must treat women as equals, with respect, and not as objects to be discarded (see 5:27-31). It's not acceptable to swear oaths in order to assure others we are telling the truth. Rather, one must be recognized as a speaker of truth (see 5:33-37). It's not enough to get along with those who are like us and who like us, but it is important to befriend the different one, the one unlike us, the one we may even consider an enemy (see 5:43-47).

The Sermon on the Mount rolls on in this fashion for three chapters; matters of prayer need to be of the heart and not performance; sharing one's offerings is a matter of the heart and not the praise of others. The message throughout is the call for consistency and integrity, a call for our lives to be transformed from within. As Jesus noted in the Sermon on the Mount, the roots and the fruits come from the same tree: "A good tree cannot bear bad fruit, nor can a bad tree bear good fruit" (Matthew 7:18). Referring to false prophets, Jesus said, "You will know them by their fruits" (7:20). Not only our behavior, but our whole being is at issue here.

This holistic approach to faith is affirmed throughout the New Testament. The letter of James states, "For just as the body without the spirit is dead, so faith without works is also dead" (James 2:26). James does not stand in opposition to the primary message of both Romans and Galatians that argues that salvation comes through faith and not works of the law (see Romans 4:2-5; Galatians 3:6-14). For Paul, faith is fundamentally trust in the promises of God that result in acts of love (see Galatians 5:6). According to Paul, the Christian faith begins with baptism, which opens the life of the believer to a "newness of life" (Romans 6:4) in which the baptized have been "set free from sin" and "have become slaves of righteousness" (6:18). Paul acknowledges that there is a mystery here, but he exhorts readers to "present your members as slaves to righteousness for sanctification" (6:19). "Members" here refers to all of one's actions and physical activities—in other words, all that one does.

James is opposed to an understanding of faith as cognitive assent to certain dogma that ignores how one actually lives. Paul understands that faith is a living interplay between mind and body that is not based on human efforts but is reflected in love. It is a faith that bears fruits of the Spirit (Galatians 5:22-25). Faith involves the totality of one's being: to love God with one's whole being and the neighbor as one would love and care for one's own self. The entire message of the Old Testament relies on these two truths (Matthew 22:36-40). Perfection is not possible, but ongoing striving is expected. As Paul writes, "I press on toward the goal for the prize of the heavenly call of God in Christ Jesus" (Philippians 3:14).

Lilly Pad Roots: The classroom of experience

The great reformers of the church such as Benedict of Clairvaux, Francis of Assisi, Martin Luther, John Calvin, John Knox, and the Wesley brothers, John and Charles, understood that the Christian faith was not merely a set of doctrines, but a way of life forged through a lifetime of wrestling with God in the midst of real, daily life experiences. These experiences led to questions and doubts as well as praise, thanksgiving, countless good works, and confidence in God's steadfast care, and no place is more conducive to honest reflection upon daily life experiences than life as it is lived in the vulnerable space of the home.

The Christian faith is not a private faith, but it is a personal faith that claims each and every follower. It is not enough to cling to the experience of individuals, but it is essential that people be able to say, with the people of Samaria, "It is no longer because of what you said that we believe, for we have heard for ourselves, and we know that this is truly the savior of the world" (John 4:42). In the deep mystery that leads people to wonder how it is that one receives and believes the word of God, the role of experience, feelings, and personal relationships cannot be ignored. Faith is captured in the midst of life experiences that make us aware of our needs and the hope that is found in the grace of God.

Croaks, Ribbits, and Hops

How can we, as adults and parents, be people through whom faith is caught by our children and youth? Certainly many habits of the heart can be established. The following ideas may trigger further strategies for you, your home, and your lifestyle.

- Identify a "faith bearer" that you know. Who teaches the faith by their actions and personhood? Have you ever told them that they are this kind of person? How did they catch the faith?
- Ask your youth and families where they are catching the faith? What are the sources?
- Talk about a time when you did not catch the faith or when you sensed it was dropped. What were the circumstances?
- As a family and congregation, go on retreats, camp outings, and service trips where children and youth can see adults "practicing" the faith themselves.
- Whom do you know who seems consistently to walk the talk? Interview him or her and ask how he or she makes their life reflect his or her values.
- Invite people of the faith to your home and ask them to tell you how they live out their faith in their work, homes, and daily lives.
- Discuss faces you remember. What made those faces memorable? Describe the faces of the people you love and from whom you have learned. What have you seen and caught in those faces? Search the pictures in magazines such as *Life*, *National Geographic*, *Time*, or *Newsweek* and look at the faces. What do the images tell you? What do you see in the eyes?
- Do a Web search on the theme "faces of Jesus," or "paintings of Jesus," and see how others have captured Jesus' face. What do you see in the various images? How would you paint Jesus' face? How would you paint his sincerity?
- Host a cross-generational Sunday school hour and ask everyone to complete the following sentence, "I caught the faith when . . ."
- Read the Sermon on the Mount together as a family and get weird with it. (W.E.I.R.D. stands for: What makes you *wonder?* What did you *experience?*

With whom did you *identify?* What did you *rediscover* about yourself? What did you *discover* about God?

NOTES

1. James Ashbrook and Carol Rausch Albright, *The Humanizing Brain* (Cleveland: The Pilgrim Press, 1997), 22.
2. Ibid., 22.
3. Ibid., 19.
4. Ibid., 21.

CHAPTER Seven

Principle 5—From Church Frogs Come Tadpoles: It takes Christian parents and other adults to raise Christian youth

Parents and many other adults powerfully shape children's lives directly or indirectly. No one can predict which adult and what circumstance will be a faith and life-shaping influence on any individual child or youth. Parents who have children by birth, marriage, adoption, or foster care know that it takes more than one or two adults to raise children; it truly takes a village. While some adults might resist the notion that they are parents for children who are not their own, the impact they can have by their actions as well as their lack of action is important. The FaithFactors team, a national, ecumenical research group based in Minneapolis, notes that at least three adults outside the home are vital to the development of Christian faith in adolescents (www.faithfactors.com). Whether adults like it or not, children and youth are watching, listening, and interpreting adult lives for the sake of their own. One can logically progress from the other four principles to this one. Since faith is formed through personal, trusted relationships, and the church is a partnership between home and congregation, and the home is church, and faith is caught, it follows that all Christian adults teach faith, values, and character formation to children and youth.

Tadpole Tale: The short left-fielder

We (the authors) have been involved (mostly unsuccessfully) in many sports activities throughout our lives—and then heading off to the clinic for much needed physical therapy! At this point in our lives we are too old to be much good, but too young to face the fact that we are not any good. What we consider exercise most observers consider comic relief. Let them laugh; we still have our dignity.

On one occasion Paul was playing softball in a church league. Church leagues tend to be extremely competitive, and often, Jesus is left in the dugout during games. Standing in left field, Paul was chatting with the short left-fielder (not a commentary on his stature; in softball each team is allowed four outfielders; the fourth is the "short left-fielder"). His name was Todd and he was a frisky, 20-something man with a reputation for wild living. Paul assumed he was playing on his team more for the love of softball than Jesus. The pastor considered Todd's involvement on the team an act of outreach and evangelism (Todd's ability to hit a ball four miles notwithstanding).

Between pitches, Todd suddenly turned around and said to Paul, a look of amazement on his face, "I'm going to be teaching seventh-grade Sunday school next year." "That's great, Todd," Paul said with forced enthusiasm. Todd went on, "Yeah, but you don't understand, I've got to clean up my act!" Paul started laughing and then Todd did too. In the meantime, a ball went sailing over their heads.

Lilly Pad Roots: Adult renewal

Todd innately understood the fifth principle; if we want Christian kids we need Christian adults. We've noted in the fourth principle that faith is caught more than taught, but something must be there for children and youth to catch. What goes on in the spiritual lives of adults does matter. Youth ministry, properly understood, is spelled *adult renewal.*

The old paradigm for youth ministry assumed that the congregation would delegate the faith formation of children and youth to a youth pastor, a youth director, or a charismatic volunteer. But one cannot hire out faith formation. The act of "faithing" the next generation is directly related to the faith formation activity that takes place in the home, the extended family, and the congregation. Again, the book of Proverbs provides insight. Written during and just after the reign of Solomon in the tenth century B.C.E., Proverbs teaches "shrewdness to the simple, knowledge and prudence to the young" (Proverbs 1:4), but significantly, is also directed to adults ("the wise"), who are to "hear and gain in learning" (1:5). Proverbs is a cross-generational teaching guide for the young based upon the spiritual character and experience of adult teachers who were often fathers, though mothers are mentioned as well. In many ways, Proverbs is a much earlier version of the catechism, acting as a teaching manual for the home that assumes that the adults in the home are themselves spiritually rooted.

One of the great passages from Proverbs that embodies the intent of catechetical instruction is 6:20-22:

> My child, keep your father's commandment, and do not forsake your mother's teaching. Bind them upon your heart always; tie them around your neck. When you walk, they will lead you; when you lie down, they will watch over you; and when you awake, they will talk with you.

These words express catechetical intent. The teaching of adults of faith guides, protects, and even talks with those instructed. What a wonderful image, and how true! All of us can recall words that were given or *fed* to us, words that shaped our lives and even engaged us in imaginary conversation, like the imaginary friends many of us have had as children. These words convey meaning, values, priorities, and a belief system that often impacts our lives on very subconscious levels. We internalize faith and values without even knowing it. Subsequently, they emerge and speak to us even before we pop out of bed in the morning. Proverbs assumes that if we are going to have faithful children and youth, faithful adults must offer instruction—the wisdom that will guide, protect, and converse with those instructed.

The central spiritual truth of Proverbs is identified early: "The fear of the LORD is the beginning of knowledge" (Proverbs 1:7). This is the message to be passed on to the next generation. Proverbs calls this Wisdom. Wisdom is understood as knowledge and insight (2:6). It is not only of the head, but of the heart as well, and as such is intended to shape the heart (2:10). The biblical understanding of *heart* means more than the seat of a person's emotions. The heart is also the location of one's intellect and volition. Therefore, the heart referred to in Proverbs really implies the center of one's being. Wisdom literally is the deepest yearning of the heart, the deepest yearnings that occur at the center of one's life. Ultimately, Wisdom shapes behavior. "Therefore walk in the way of the good, and keep to the paths of the just. For the upright will abide in the land . . ." (2:20). Wisdom embraces the whole person: the thoughts, knowledge, heart, and behavior of the individual. To live faithfully in the "fear of the LORD" is the Wisdom that touches every part of our lives. As we respect, honor, trust, revere, and rely on God we live "in fear of the LORD"; we live with Wisdom.

Wisdom is about the whole character transformation of the adult, youth, and child, but often, the parameters of wisdom are limited to the imparting of information, especially if the information helps control or direct behavior. Parenting, for example, often involves such "wisdom." The logistics of the household, such as boundary setting ("You'll be in by 11:00 P.M.") or travel arrangements for the family taxi, help run a household but do little to transform the character of family members. Or consider skill-based camps for youth. Children are sent to basketball camp, band camp, computer camp, or cheerleader camp. These are wonderful opportunities that expose them to new things and help them learn new skills, but such instruction never asks the most important question, "How can camp *transform* the lives of children and youth?" How can adults touch the hearts, indeed, the entire beings of children with the fear of the LORD—with Wisdom?

Tadpole Tale: Called by God

Paul is a former church camp director. The outdoor ministries of the church transform lives, most particularly 20-year-old college students who often serve as camp counselors. For years, Paul reviewed literally thousands of camper evaluations. When asked, "What was the most important part of camp for you?" more than 90 percent of evaluations cited the relationship established with the cabin counselor as most significant.

One junior high youth reported to his parents that his camp counselor, Jim, was going to go to seminary. The parents responded politely. The youth spoke up again, "No Mom, you don't understand, Jim has been called by God. He's doing it because of God." The mother was surprised and pleased with her young son's enthusiasm and reported to the camp director, "Whatever is inside Jim just got inside my son." This is deeply rooted transformation, the beginning of Wisdom.

Lilly Pad Roots: Proverbs is a cross-generational journey book

Proverbs lifts up the importance of the cross-generational nature of Wisdom sharing. Spiritual adults transform the next generation through many generations and for many generations. Proverbs 4 begins,

> Listen, children, to a father's instruction, and be attentive, that you may gain insight; for I give you good precept: do not forsake my teaching. *When I was a son with my father tender, and my mother's favorite, he taught me, and said to me,* "Let your heart hold fast my words; keep my commandments and live. Get wisdom."

Wisdom is passed on across many generations because of the spiritual nature of the grandfather who passed it on to the father who passed it on to the son who will pass it on to his son. (Although Proverbs was written in a time when the focus was more on men and sons, the wisdom provided by this book is, of course, intended in our day for women as well.)

Wisdom contains a specific behavioral content. How we live, our ethics and manner of behaving, is a significant reflection of Wisdom and is observed by the young. Proverbs writes,

> There are six things that the LORD hates, seven that are an abomination to him: haughty eyes, a lying tongue, and hands that shed blood, a heart that devises wicked plans, feet that hurry to run to evil, a lying witness who testifies falsely, and one who sows discord in a family (Proverbs 6:6).

Proverbs weaves together "fear of the LORD" and suitable moral and ethical behavior. Spiritual centering and moral conduct are of the same fabric, threads inextricably bound together. Lose one thread and the other unravels as well.

At the present time, the United States is rapidly building prisons to warehouse our youth. We house more people in our prisons than any other industrial nation. Younger and younger children are bullying, intimidating, or shooting their classmates. The cry is for tougher and tougher laws. The direction of the courts is to try more of them as adults. As adults we need to question this strategy and look within ourselves. Could it be that a desert exists *within us,* a vast empty spiritual dryness that the young have discovered? We have filled the spiritual void in our lives with things, entertainment thrills, consumer habits, and exotic vacations and yet we are still empty. The kids know it, and for some this is acted out in reprehensible behavior. Being a Christian parent, pastor, youth worker, volunteer, mentor, Sunday school teacher, instructor, choir leader, godparent, or peer minister is all about one's own spiritual life—a life to be shared with others.

Tadpole Tale: "Y'all need to witness!"

One of our former students, now serving as a youth minister in Texas, shared this story. After having completed her training with us, she headed back to her congregation with great excitement, energy, and a plan in hand. We caught up with her a year later and asked how it was going. She said, "Well, there's a lot of stuff I learned from y'all (did we mention she's from Texas?) that I haven't used yet. And there are lots of things that I tried that didn't work. But there is one thing that stands out above everything else that I have tried. In fact, this one thing is the best thing you taught me. We do occasional cross-generational Sunday schools and we ask our adults to share their witness with the kids. Everyone loves it."

Lily Pad Roots: The teachable moment

This youth worker rediscovered the truth of the teachable moment. Teachable moments in faith transmission take place when children are curious and ask questions of spiritual adults regarding the importance of the Christian faith. Deuteronomy reflects upon these occasions and offers a parental reply:

> When your children ask you in time to come, "What is the meaning of the decrees and the statues and the ordinances that the LORD our God has commanded you?" then you shall say to your children, "We were Pharaoh's slaves in Egypt, but the LORD brought us out of Egypt with a mighty hand. The LORD displayed before our eyes great and awesome signs and wonders against Egypt, against Pharaoh and all his household" (Deuteronomy 6:20-22).

Four things are to be noted here. First, the children's question is formed in such a way that the focus is on the faith of the adults, not the children. The children could be asking, "What does this stuff mean to you, Grandma?" The concern identified by the children is how the faith makes a difference to adult lives. In essence, the children are wondering what it is about this adult faith that should interest or make a claim on them as well.

Second, the answer to be given is not a rational discourse on the objective, social value of the decrees, statutes, and ordinances. The relevance of the faith is documented in the form of faith stories. Adults are to respond by sharing how God first made a difference in their lives. The value of the decrees, statutes, and ordinances is based on what God had already done for them. First God delivered, and "then the LORD commanded us to observe all these statutes" (Deuteronomy 6:24). The value of following the teachings and lifestyle of the faith is a consequence of the relationship already established with God and by God.

Third, the adult tells the faith story in such a way that children see it as their story as well. All generations take on the biblical story as their own story. All subsequent generations of adults and children take on the biblical story as their own story. It is the story of transformation from slavery to freedom.

Fourth, adults are seen as the teachers of the faith tradition. Deuteronomy 11:2 makes this point most emphatically.

> Remember today that it was not your children (who have not known or seen the discipline of the LORD your God), but it is you who must acknowledge his greatness, his mighty hand and his outstretched arm.

Adults, not children, are those who are called upon to give witness to faith in God. Adults are the ones with the memory of an experience with the living God that must be shared. Once again the message is that faith is formed and passed on through personal, trusted relationships—often relationships within one's own household, and it is spiritual adults who plant seeds of faith in spiritual kids.

Lily Pad Roots: The importance of adult education

This conclusion is supported in a statistical analysis[1] of the levels of participation in Christian education at various stages of life in different denominations: the Christian Church (Disciples of Christ), Evangelical Lutheran Church in America (ELCA), Presbyterian Church (U.S.A.), United Church of Christ, United Methodist Church, and the Southern Baptist Convention.

	TOTAL	CC	ELCA	PC	UCC	UMC	SBC
Children grades K-6	60	61	67	69	66	56	48
Youth grades 7-9	52	55	70	48	54	45	52
Youth grades 10-12	35	47	32	40	33	35	49
Adults	28	35	23	31	22	29	49

The study does not try to evaluate the quality of the education, but offers a quantitative analysis of how many are present for education. Note the constant drop in the levels of participation from elementary school age through adulthood. A loss of participation happens at each stage, especially after grades seven through nine.

The ELCA experience gives some of the most revealing data. From grades seven through nine, the ELCA has the highest level of participation among any of the six denominations studied, and the greatest differentiation between its percentage of participation and that of the other denominations. Yet, after grades seven through nine, the ELCA goes from having the highest percentage of education participants to the lowest percentage in grades 10 through 12 (from 70 percent to 32 percent). Once ELCA youth complete confirmation (generally the educational cornerstone of grades seven through nine in Lutheran churches), they drop out at a greater rate than any other denominational group studied. In the adult category, the ELCA bottoms out with the UCC for the lowest levels of participation (23 percent and 22 percent, respectively).

High school youth see themselves approaching adulthood. What ELCA youth have modeled for them in their denomination is a low rate of adult involvement in Christian education. For ELCA youth, to model ELCA adulthood is to be relatively inactive in Christian education. ELCA high school youth reflect adult inactivity through low levels of participation.

The ELCA findings are far different from the Southern Baptists. The levels of participation never soar as high as ELCA numbers, but neither do the Southern Baptists fall off the edge of the educational precipice. Their high school youth are involved at a level of 49 percent and their adults are involved at a level of 49 percent. Southern Baptist youth see a much higher level of education participation in the adults, and the youth appear to respond to this modeling with a level of participation that is high compared with the other denominations.

This pattern underscores the basic premise of nurturing the faith lives of children and youth: modeling is essential. Faith is caught more than it is taught, and parents and other significant adults in their lives spread the faith and values caught by children and youth.

Tadpole Tale: Mom and Dad in the kitchen

One youth leader tells the story of how he discovered faith was significant. He grew up poor on a farm in South Dakota. The work was very hard and the economy was abysmal. One day he came running into the house for lunch. Usually it was a bustling, noisy place with his mother preparing the meal while everybody washed up. However, on this day, it was quiet in the house. He had come in a bit early and stepped into the living area to discover both his parents on their knees praying together. He heard their prayer, too. They told God they were poor and that life was getting very hard. The struggle for survival was getting to a critical juncture. They asked God for mercy and help. This future leader was deeply impacted by this experience. Being young, he had no idea of the extent of their economic troubles. He had never thought of himself as poor. Prayer was a common practice in his home, but usually around meals or bedtime. To see his parents on their knees praying in the middle of the day calling upon God for help was transformational.

Lily Pad Roots: Popular culture drives a wedge between the generations

We can rediscover the power of our own spiritual journey and share it in significant ways with the next generation. We will do this, however, in the context of a culture that wishes to separate the generations into niches based upon age, race, and income demographics. For example, advertisers operate on the assumption that children become consumers by age three. Several billions of dollars in advertising are spent annually targeting such age groups as four- to 12-year-olds.[2] And this investment in advertising works. The teen consumer market represents $150 billion dollars![3]

To be effective, consumer capitalism works to identify markets or niches. This is not necessarily evil in itself. Through niche marketing, items are sold, money is earned, and the economy is sustained. However, in order for consumer capitalism to be successful, the culture must be segregated. The generations are divided into almost every imaginable construct, including music, clothes, diet, vacation preferences, even sex habits.

B. Earl Puckett, former president of a department store conglomerate, noted, "It is our job to make people unhappy with what they have."[4] With the assistance of the advertising industry, our consumer culture exploits this unhappiness to make people desire more. People are conditioned to want what they don't have and be dissatisfied with what they do have. How family friendly is that? This climate creates an atmosphere in the home that fosters unhappiness that can only be resolved through purchases rather than healthy relationships.

Tadpole Tale: Dad in the school hallway

A closely related dynamic also contributes to the demise of adult mentoring of the lives of children and youth: an anti-parent sentiment. It isn't cool to like one's parents—at least not publicly. As Mary Pipher writes in *The Shelter of Each Other,* "In our culture, after a certain age, children no longer have permission to love their parents. We define adulthood as breaking away, disagreeing and making up new rules. Just when teenagers most need their parents, they are encouraged to distance from them."[5]

When one of our daughters entered the fifth grade, dad could no longer hold her hand in public. It wasn't okay for dad's "little girl" to show such affection. In the ninth grade, this same daughter called dad to come to school to pick up her downhill skis since the school's skiing trip had been called off. Dad was eager to help and be at the school just as the students were being dismissed. Dad got the skis and waited to give his daughter a ride home. The daughter approached dad from down the hallway. For a moment their eyes meet, but only for a brief moment. As the daughter approached dad she walked by him as though she had not seen him at all. In mock shock and with humiliating delight, Dad yelled out, "Kirsten, it's your dad, don't you remember me?" It's not easy being a cool teen, but sometimes it can be fun being a nerdy dad.

Lily Pad Root: The culture of adolescence

The culture, in short, does not intend to foster spiritual adults nor does it intend for adults/parents to connect with the younger generations in a mentoring role. Rather, the culture emphasizes youthfulness and encourages in adults a perpetual adolescence in young and old alike. Our culture values youthfulness but not youth. Nearly everyone wants the energy, vitality, looks, athleticism, and sparkle of youth, but we are impatient with the turmoil, the searching, the relational struggles, the awkwardness, and the self-consciousness of adolescence. Because we want youthfulness and devalue youth, we fail to mature. Not surprisingly, the faith maturity of half of all men in their 40s is not that different than that of adolescent youth.[6] Gene Roehlkepartain reports in *The Teaching Church* that only 32 percent of U.S. Christians have a mature faith.[7]

Not surprisingly, given this lack of adult faith maturity, one-third of mainline Protestant adults believe that "through meditation and self-discipline I come to know that all spiritual truth and wisdom is within me"[8] a decidedly un-Christian theology, but appropriate to a consumer culture that worships individual cravings at any cost.

Roehlkepartain offers four suggestions that fit well into the principles regarding spiritual adults.

a) Christian education . . . must involve people of mature faith nurturing others.[9] (Principle 1: Faith is formed through personal, trusted relationships; and Principle 5: It takes Christian parents and other adults to raise Christian children and youth.)

b) Christian education should reclaim strategies that include sharing stories, individual and small group conversations, service projects, and the involvement of parents. Technology is not the whole answer.[10] (Principle 3: The home is church, too; and Principle 4: Faith is caught more than it is taught.)

c) New models of Christian education must be discovered.[11] (The Four Keys promote an environment for faith formation that can be developed in a rich variety of settings.)

d) Christian education must be viewed holistically, not as a separate entity.[12] (Principle 2: The church is a partnership between the ministry of the home and the ministry of the congregation.)

Maturity is a real issue in our consumer-based and individualistic (read: isolated and lonely) culture. Our society has not valued a sense of the common good, commitment to others, sacrifice, and mentoring. These character-forming social commitments all too often are missing. Of course, many individuals have risen to the occasion with wonderful acts of selfless service to others, but this generally is not valued as a societal norm. However, these are essential ingredients to an adult life that pursues mature contributions to the welfare of others rather than more trips, toys, and tabloid affairs of one sort or another.

If we are to have faithful children and adults, we need adults committed to the care, the grooming, and the development of younger generations. We subscribe to the notion that we tend not to have good adult-child relationships because it is sometimes difficult to tell the two apart. Adults need to grow and mature as citizens of society as well as citizens of the kingdom of God.

Croaks, Ribbits, and Hops

The Center for Youth Ministries at Wartburg Seminary offers a three-week training school in youth and family ministry called Certification School. Congregations send lay leaders, volunteers, and youth ministers to this school to develop youth and family ministry skills for the twenty-first century.

As a part of the preparation to attend, a pre-Certification School interview is held with a group of people from the congregation sending the student. This group includes the pastor, the council president, youth, other lay leaders, and the prospective student. In this interview we give six assignments to the congregation that will help facilitate effective faith formative practices. We now suggest that *every* congregation do these six things as a way of implementing this principle.

1. Ask and train every council member to do daily devotions in their own lives. If they are spiritually journeying then they are leading by example.
2. Ask every council member to make a point of connecting to the life of one young person. They role model a cross-generational lifestyle.
3. Provide council time to develop a vision and design for ministry based upon the Five Principles and Four Keys. This means they are studying, discerning, and prioritizing.
4. Commission those who are coming to Certification School in a formal worship setting. This lifts up the value of leaders and their gifts.

5. Create a cross-generational group of people who will pray for their leaders while away at training. They need to pray together at least once a week. This models cross-generational witnessing and prayer.
6. Join a youth ministry network. This models the importance of ongoing education, inspiration, and the corporate nature of this important work. "Lone Rangers" are not effective leaders.

These six habits of the whole church frog will help enormously in developing mature, spiritual adults who nurture the next generation in the faith.

- Sit down with family or close friends and determine what it is that makes you unhappy. Make another list of blessings in your life. Compare the two lists. Does that which makes you unhappy really have power over your sense of self and peace and joy in life? Could it be that you have been deceived by a consumer-based society to be forever unhappy, to have an insatiable desire for more goods and services? Consider what it is that gives you peace, joy, and the sensation that your life is truly blessed. The historic prayer service before retiring at night is called Compline. The word *compline* means complete. What is it about the Christian life that allows you to lay your head on the pillow at night and retire with an awareness that your life is complete?

- For the sake of inoculating yourself against "consumer fever," listen to radio and watch television commercials and sitcoms with an ear to the messages sent about happiness. Also evaluate how parents or older generations are portrayed compared to children and youth. Are the adults perceived as elders to be venerated and emulated, or as oafs who are out of touch? How are children and youth perceived? Are they seen as valued and competent people or as something less? If something less, what children or youth characteristics are portrayed in the media?

- How do your family and congregation portray children, youth, and adults? Who is valued for their contributions to the common good of the church and society? Make lists for the various generations and the assumptions made about these people. Are they positive? Could your family, friends, and congregation make changes in attitudes that value all people at all ages? How can you be a part of various communities that benefit from the contributions of all the generations?

NOTES

1. *Effective Christian Education: A National Study of Protestant Congregations—A Report for the Evangelical Lutheran Church in America* (Minneapolis: Search Institute, 1990), 53.

2. David Walsh, *Selling Out America's Children,* 42.

3. *Merchants of Cool, Frontline,* PBS, 1999.

4. David Walsh, *Selling Out America's Children,* 39.

5. Mary Pipher, *The Shelter of Each Other: Rebuilding Our Families* (New York: Ballantine Books, 1996), 24.

6. Gene Roehlkepartain, *The Teaching Church: Moving Christian Education to Center Stage* (Nashville: Abingdon, 1993), 38.

7. Ibid., 19.

8. Ibid., 45.

9. Ibid., 11.

10. Ibid., 12.

11. Ibid., 12.

12. Ibid., 12.

CHAPTER EIGHT

Let's All Do the Hop: Four Keys to nurturing faith in the home and congregation

Much of the world changed on September 11, 2001. The Twin Towers of the World Trade Center collapsed under terrorist attack, the Pentagon burned, and a hijacked airplane crashed into Pennsylvania farmland. The days and weeks following this unimaginable event captured the attention of the whole world.

Americans responded to their shock, grief, anger, and sadness in countless ways. Volunteers drove thousands of miles to help assist in the aftermath of the attack. Others gave blood, money, food, clothing, and even offered their homes to those affected. Counselors, pastors, doctors, and strangers on the street became the voice and ears of compassion for a hurting nation. Congregations, synagogues, mosques, and temples opened their doors and offered religious spaces for prayer vigils, worship services, candlelight gatherings, and other opportunities for people to experience a sense of the divine. Spontaneous shrines emerged at ground zero, at the Pennsylvania crash site, near the Pentagon, and at many other locations associated with the lives of the victims. Such memorials offered numerous occasions for pause and prayer. In Washington, D.C., mourners walked the streets in silence carrying candles in an impromptu parade of grief and determination. The march not only expressed the deep sense of loss, it fortified and unified people seeking the courage to face an unknown future.

Most significant were the numerous funerals of fire fighters, emergency medical personnel, and police officers. These funerals, especially those of the fire fighters, were deeply embedded in rituals unbeknownst to most outsiders until this time. The wailing of bagpipes filled the air. Surviving firefighters and their families visited the homes of the bereaved. Emergency financial relief was made available to victims' families. The New York City mayor and the state governor personally attended many of these funerals. Color guards marched and firefighters wore full dress uniforms, while athletes and celebrities wore black bands. Firehouses and police precincts were draped in black shrouds and American flags. In fact, throughout the United States, flags were flown at half-mast and displayed on cars, homes, stores, front lawns, freeway signs, and overpasses. Lit candles expressed a mixture of grief, hope, and solidarity.

Four responses emerged in the wake of this tragedy. First, citizens came together around caring conversations with one another. Second, spiritual renewal emerged through public and personal expressions of various faith traditions and practices. Third, Americans generously reached out to one another with compassionate service in ways not witnessed for decades. Finally, people across America drew sustenance and courage out of grief for a fearful future by relying on rituals and traditions that were deeply imbedded in the culture.

These four distinct yet inseparable responses to grief and a search for understanding and community are developed in this section as the Four Keys. Rarely have a people so clearly and dramatically given testimony to the critical and basic practices of the spiritual life that are foundational to human existence. What follows are further reflections on the significance and power of the Four Keys, so clearly illustrated on and following September 11 and critically important and effective in the life of the church.

Lily Pad Roots: The cycle of life and the search for meaning

Whenever a child is born, someone, probably a parent, wonders, "How will the baby grow up in this world? Will the little one be safe? Will she find happiness? Will he find something to believe in? Will she feel secure and have a sense of purpose? Will he find love?" Indeed, many will wonder how they can be a positive influence in a child's life. For instance, when a young person leaves home to be on her own, those who have been near to give support and care wonder, "What will happen now in the life of this person? What have I given him over the years to anchor his life, to give him a compass, to help him set his course with faith, hope, and love?" Adults will ask, "Have I done enough? Where could I have done more? What have I forgotten to offer as a guide along the way? Some may even ask themselves, What are the guides, the resources, the tools for mentoring, anyway?"

When someone is at that rare moment of knowing he or she has reached the end of life and wonders what it all has meant, what difference that person has made, and what hope still lies ahead, the pondering occurs again: "Has my life made a difference? What did I contribute? What is there to fear? What is there to have as hope? Who will remember me and for what?" At this moment in time, "How can my life and my death be a source of faith, hope, and love?"

These are precious and powerful moments, but they are moments that should not be left to isolated individuals to wrestle with alone. These are the tough and passionate questions of life that need a response from a community of care; a community that equips and supports, prays for, and serves one another. These are the occasions of life that remind us of the importance and the value of a full-bodied church in which disciples of Jesus are made.

The Five Principles of faith formation for the full-bodied church frog offer a foundation for understanding how the community of care and meaning impacts individual lives and the larger world. We now turn our attention to specific ways the full-bodied church frog hops and croaks in the world to shape lives. What we now propose are four basic ways of encountering the world and one another and of leaving an imprint that marks truth, honor, justice, purity, pleasure, and commendation—the things that are worthy of praise (see Philippians 4:8).

These four basic ways of interacting with God, others, and the creation are referred to as the Four Keys. The Four Keys include: 1. caring conversation, 2. devotional life, 3. service, and 4. rituals and traditions. These four basic activities of the life of faith honor and help develop the legs of the church frog, legs that give mobility and vitality to the ministry of the church. The Four Keys are the habits of the Christian heart that bring the Five Principles to life. They enable individuals, homes, congregations, and other settings for Christian community to be nurtured and strengthened in, and challenged and delighted by the Christian faith.

The Four Keys are basic disciplines of faithful Christians living in the first or the twenty-first century. They represent foundational practices of life that, shaped by the good news of Jesus Christ, strengthen faith in daily life. That is, they keep the church frog legs from being neglected and experiencing atrophy. The Four Keys serve what the church calls the "means of grace"—avenues for the work of the Holy Spirit to create faith and build the church, the body of Christ. The Four Keys help the church in the congregation and the church in the home make people "acquainted with the gospel," in the language of Martin Luther.

These key practices of the Christian faith respond to the exhortation in Ephesians to "lead a life worthy of the calling to which you have been called, with all humility and gentleness, with patience, bearing with one another in love, making every effort to maintain the unity of the Spirit in the bond of peace" (4:1-3, see also 1 Corinthians 9:24-25; Philippians 1:27; 3:12-16; Colossians 1:9-10, 28-29; 1 Thessalonians 2:12). Ephesians 4 goes on to express concern that the whole body be "knit together by every ligament with which it is equipped, as each part is working properly, promotes the body's growth in building itself up in love" (verse 16). The Four Keys are foundational ways that the church is "knit together" by the work of the Holy Spirit.

Now that the image of the church frog with legs has been established, we will explore how the church functions as a fully connected body. Through a description of the Four Keys, what follows presents an understanding of how we grow in Christ and strengthen the body of Christ; of how we share the gospel with stranger, family, and friend alike. The Four Keys impact the leadership of the church frog head by guiding church leaders with a vision of the church that is more than effective programs that bring people "to church." The Four Keys also influence the gathering of the church frog torso by contributing specific goals and activities that strengthen the church outside the public gathering of the Christian community. Finally, the Four Keys give concrete expression to the life of the church in daily life, equipping the church frog legs to hop and move so that the church can more effectively pass on the Christian faith and life to all generations.

Lily Pad Roots: The creative Spirit

A way of thinking of the Four Keys is to think about what generates life. One could take all the elements necessary for life such as carbon, hydrogen, oxygen, amino acids, and so on, and mix them together but still not create life. For life to happen energy must be infused into this chemical soup. Energy creates the unique molecular bonds that make up life. For the Christian, the Holy Spirit is the energy that creates the life of faith. How that life of faith is lived out and expressed is described in terms of faith practices or disciplines. The Four Keys represent our formulation of foundational faith practices out of which a rich variety of faith life emerges.

We want to be clear, however, that it is *the Spirit* that brings life to the basic elements of the Five Principles and Four Keys. When speaking of faith practices, this fundamental point can get lost. People can and often do miss the point that faith and the life of faith are the work and will of God. The Holy Spirit makes Christ and the Christian life a present reality for people. Through the Holy Spirit, the personal, Trinitarian God moves out of history lessons and theological speculation to be the God who is with us here and now in daily life (see Romans 8, especially verses 9-11). Christian disciplines described through the Four Keys are ways to be open to the work of the Spirit in the lives of individuals and communities. They are not ways to control or manipulate God, but are ways to be open to God's life-giving, redeeming, and sustaining activity in the larger world and our personal lives. The Four Keys offer a way of being receptive to the work and will of God. In other words, the Word and Spirit of God come to us through such activities as caring conversation, devotions, service, and rituals and traditions.

Perhaps the biggest drawback to such activity is its simplicity and lack of spiritual pizzazz—no necessary glamour, no required drama. Let's face it, who would have written the divine script to focus on a virgin birth to a poor couple without a forwarding address? Who would have made a painful, criminal's death the moment of divine glory? Who would have made Jesus' life the biography for all time? He ate with sinners and tax collectors; he angered religious leaders and confused his own followers; he delighted the needy, the poor, the not-so-famous, the forgotten; he elevated the common and the vulgar, and lowered those with pedigrees (see Luke 1:46-55). The marvel, the miracle, the mystery, and that which defies religious sensitivities is that God enters into our lives through such mundane activities as talking, reflecting, serving, celebrating, and remembering. At times these things may seem dull, but they may be the least-expected occasions through which lives become awash with a sense of God's presence. This is the Christianity and Christian practice that is at the center of the life of the church, whether it be the church in the home, the congregation, or the larger community.

Many faith practices have been developed in the church through the centuries, and we applaud them. Indeed, faith practices permeate the history and life of the church for the purpose of strengthening Christian life; practices such as the monastic life, Twelve Step recovery programs, or denominational discipleship efforts. We choose to focus on the Four Keys because we have found that organizing the life of congregations and homes around a larger list makes it nearly impossible to use such diverse practices as guides for life and faith. The wisdom of the Four Keys is its capacity to include a wide variety of faith practices within simple, inclusive, and memorable categories. The Four Keys also serve as points of reference from which more detailed faith disciplines can be developed.

Lily Pad Root: From where do the Four Keys come?

Modern research as well as Scripture and church history have identified the importance of the Four Keys in the life of the church. The Search Institute, in its study *Effective Christian Education: A Summary Report,* concluded the following:

> Of the two strongest connections to faith maturity, family religiousness is slightly more important than lifetime exposure to Christian education. The particular family experiences most tied to greater faith maturity are the frequency with which an adolescent talked with mother and father about faith, the frequency of family devotions, and the frequency with which parents and children together were involved in efforts, formal or informal, to help other people. Each of these family experiences is more powerful than the frequency with which an adolescent sees his or her parents engage in religious behavior like church attendance.[1]

This and similar research on the faith and character formation of youth identify how the home life itself plays a critical role (see www.faithfactors.com). Homes that were able to make a significant difference in the lives of children and youth in areas such as faith, values, and character formation were homes that engaged in conversation, devotions, and service. Thus, we have three of the four practices of the Four Keys.

The other practice, rituals and traditions, is noted in family theory and therapy. Family rituals and traditions convey material that says a lot about individual families. What families choose to celebrate and how they celebrate experientially articulates what a family believes and values. The routines that a family follows (either consciously chosen or implicitly adopted over time) reveal important information about the content of their lives—their hopes, dreams, and convictions.

The Scriptures are filled with examples of traditions, rituals, and customs that guide the lives of God's people. The church in its worship and daily life is also embedded with identifiable rituals and traditions. This is even true of contemporary church bodies that seem to disdain traditions and rituals. They have simply substituted new ones for older, established ones, oral rituals for written and codified traditions. For example, mainline denominations routinely follow a liturgical outline in worship practice that has deep historical roots, and is often written down. The free church traditions, by contrast, often follow a liturgical format that is understood by everyone gathered for worship, yet rarely written down explicitly. The point is, no matter the tradition, each faith community has rituals, traditions, and language woven into its worship life.

The Four Keys not only apply to the life of the home, but also the life of the congregation. A devotional life exists for households and also for the more public devotional life of the congregation experienced in worship services. Families often express their devotedness to God primarily through congregational worship. For the entire church frog to hop and move effectively, individuals and groups need to worship and devote themselves to God's living Word in the more personal arena of the home as well as the more public sphere of the congregation. Likewise, caring conversations, service, and rituals and traditions are meant to be experienced both in the home and the congregation.

Lily Pad Roots: Don't go linear
The temptation to think of the Four Keys in a linear way needs to be resisted. Prioritizing the Four Keys misses the organic and cyclical relationship they have with each other. To engage in one Key often leads to or includes another of the Keys. For example, while doing family devotions in the home it's quite possible that caring conversation will take place as well. The act of doing daily devotions in the home becomes, in and of itself, a ritual or tradition. Engaging in daily devotions in the home actually touches upon three of the Four Keys.

A woman was visiting her brother and his family. One evening she joined the rest of the family for their regular devotional time. The devotional theme related to being a servant in the kingdom of God. At the conclusion of the devotion the woman's niece uncharacteristically picked up her dishes and took them to the sink. The girl's brother asked what she was doing. She responded, "Didn't you just hear? We are servants in the kingdom of God." The brother answered back, "No silly, we are not part of the kingdom of God until we die." The aunt interjected that perhaps they needed some more conversation about the meaning of the kingdom of God. Within this story we find all Four Keys: family devotions held regularly (rituals and traditions) that led to caring conversation (reflections on the kingdom of God), and an act of service (bussing dishes).

Think of the Four Keys as threads within a woven fabric. Together the threads create a pattern or perhaps even a picture or image. To pull one thread out of the cloth would leave a discernable gap in the material and the pattern would be disrupted. All the threads working in concert are needed to make up the design. The Four Keys work like the threads. Woven together they form a strong cloth and pattern.

Attention to the Four Keys provides an effective way to partner the ministry of the congregation with the ministry and life of the home. The Keys serve as ways to receive and communicate the message and the life of the Christian faith, not in an isolated but integrative fashion.

A common concern that arises when working with adults on the topic of nurturing the faith in the home is that what is transmitted is not only a relationship to God, but also an enriched relationship with one another. As one congregational president and parent of two youth said, "What I want is not only to have faith in my home, but also good relationships with my kids." He was looking for something from his congregation that would impact the quality of the daily life of his home, and not only eternal hope and comfort for his children.

This parent expressed an often-stated and often-felt filial passion. Parents want warm and open relationships with their children and grandchildren. Friends, spouses, mentors, and others involved in personal relationships want a way of life that shares the life and message of Christ and fosters deep personal ties. Jesus called his followers friends. He prayed for their unity, for their common mission in life. To follow Jesus through such practices as caring conversation, devotions, service, and rituals and traditions, is to follow the One who binds people together in sacrificial love, the kind that renews, enlivens, and celebrates a common future.

Lily Pad Roots: Four Key everything!

The Four Keys offer an effective, doable strategy for congregations wishing to develop a meaningful and faith-focused partnership between home and congregation. A fundamental goal of congregational leadership is to routinely edify children, youth, and adults and equip them with at least one of the Four Key activities. Whether it be worship, Christian education, fellowship time, evangelism, stewardship, or even property management, those who are gathered can be sent forth with a conversation starter, a devotional suggestion, an idea or two for cross-generational service, or a way to recall God's word by incorporating a ritual or tradition. The church seasons, the Bible texts being studied at the time, or a theme being emphasized within the congregation could easily be connected to one or more of the Four Keys for people to take with them into their daily lives.

Even—perhaps especially—preaching can include the Four Keys. While teaching one congregation the vision of the church frog with legs, the pastor was encouraged to find the Four Keys in the texts he used for preaching. He responded with a sense of panic. He had never been taught to do this in his seminary training. It had not been part of his practice. We simply asked him to consider locating as many of the Four Keys as possible and imagine ways to incorporate them into his preaching. We also offered to help him explore this process in his preaching in the weeks ahead, but he never called for that assistance. Once he looked at his sermon texts, he discovered how easy it was to identify and reflect upon the story of faith through conversations taking place, through reflective and prayerful attention to God's word, through a life of loving service, and through symbols, gestures, routines, and other forms of rituals and traditions that enlivened the awareness of God's presence through Christ Jesus in the lives of both past and present disciples.

Through the conscious application of the Four Keys, the ministry that takes place when people gather together publicly becomes the source of ongoing edification for their daily lives and relationships. The Four Keys also strengthen and clarify the corporate life and witness of the congregation and larger church. That witness enters into the community more vigorously through the homes that incorporate the Four Keys. The ministry of the home and the ministry of the congregation strengthen each other. This symbiotic relationship nurtures faith more effectively. No longer limited to the pews, pulpits, or other formal marks of the congregation, the good news of Jesus Christ now has an infinite variety of ways to be heard, sensed, and received by people day in and day out—both in and out of congregation and home.

Lily Pad Roots: Biblical perspectives

The Scriptures are full of admonitions to live the faith in the concrete, visible ways exemplified by the Four Keys. As an adult mentor of a young man, the apostle Paul said to Timothy,

> Let no one despise your youth, but set the believers an example in speech and conduct, in love, in faith, in purity. Until I arrive, give attention to the public reading of scripture, to exhorting, to teaching . . . Put these things into practice, devote yourself to them, so that all may see your progress (1 Timothy 4:11-13, 15).

Paul identified the Four Keys! Or rather, the Four Keys can be found in Paul's teachings:

1. Caring conversation: "set the believers an example in speech"
2. Family devotions: "give attention to . . . exhorting and teaching, put these things into practice, devote yourself . . ."
3. Service: "set the believers an example . . . in love"
4. Rituals and traditions: "give attention to the public reading of Scripture"

These are the disciplines of the whole church frog. Living the Four Keys in home and congregation is as faith formative today as it was in the time of the New Testament church.

Tadpole Tale: Are you religious or spiritual?

Today's generations address the spirituality behind these faith practices from a different perspective: the distinction made between religion and spirituality. This distinction is evident in one young adult's question to his pastor father. The 28-year-old son came home for a visit and asked, "Dad, I know you are religious, but are you spiritual?" The question caught the father off guard. His life had been immersed in congregational leadership marked by Christian devotion to public worship, education, fellowship, and service. For the father, his Christian faith clearly shaped both his personal and public life. To the son, it was not so clear. Dad's loyalty and activity linked to a congregation was not enough evidence that Dad's life was grounded in a daily experience with a living God. The son was looking for a life of faith evidenced in unconventional (read: non-congregational) settings.

In another cross-generational conversation, a middle-aged woman entered an ice-cream parlor to order some frozen yogurt. She happened to be wearing a cross on a necklace. The young man serving her behind the counter commented on how beautiful her cross was. After admiring it for a few moments, he looked at her and asked, "Do you practice?" He assumed there was a difference between wearing attractive jewelry and being a Christian. He wanted to know if the cross was simply part of a particular ensemble that combined clothing with certain accessories, or if it signified something more. The young man's question was not simply, "Do you go to church?" or "Are you a Christian." It was more specific than that. He wanted to know, "Do you practice?"

The woman was flustered by the question. She was not exactly sure how to answer. She rephrased the question in her mind to ask, "Are you a Christian?" After gathering her thoughts together she simply answered, "Yes, I go to church." But the question continued to be unsettling for her. She wanted to say more, but she was not sure at that moment what else to say. She sensed that stating her first thought—that she attended church—was not enough to satisfy the young man behind the counter. The question, "Do you practice?" was more than a question of allegiance to a particular religious label or community. The question probes deeper than that. "Do you practice?" investigates whether or not there is a particular conviction and lifestyle associated with the religious symbol of a cross.

Lily Pad Roots: It's not either/or but both/and

The woman wearing the cross had not consciously thought of her Christian faith in terms of practice but of a belief system that led her to a life with others in a congregational setting. It was not that she did not live or practice her faith daily, but initially she had not thought of her Christianity in those terms. Older generations tend to identify with the "practices" or "traditions" of their congregation and larger church. Younger generations tend to question such identification, preferring to see authentic Christianity (or any other religion) in terms that are experienced personally and less motivated by activities associated with an institutional religious body. For the older, more church-going generations, traditions and congregational activities and routines are good; personal experiences and practices are not necessarily bad, just not part of their frame of reference when thinking about the Christian faith. For the younger generations who tend to question institutional life, traditions and organizational patterns are not enough; a personal spirituality motivated by a living faith and not external forces is expected.

These two worlds are not so far apart. What is needed is a bridge to link two perspectives. The life of the baptized can take place in the larger world of the public church and can reach into one's daily life of the home. The one perspective is observed from the corporate while the other from the personal point of view. The one sees from the vantage point of a life grounded in congregational worship and related activities while the other lacks that perspective. Instead, the younger generations search for what is real and meaningful. They tend to be less attached to and even more suspicious of institutional, denominational, and congregational life. The one view is simply more comfortable identifying the Christian life through the public gathering of Christians, but Christian activities such as prayer, Scripture reading, and service are still assumed to be part of one's daily life. In fact, people who are active in congregations often articulate a clear desire to bring the faith home and express an awareness that something is missing if faith is only about participating in congregational worship or some other "church" activity. The pastor father of the 28-year-old would likely have listed prayer, Scripture reading, and service as part of his personal Christian practice, but would not necessarily have understood these home activities as part of "church." Rather, they were simply things that faithful people do.

Tadpole Tale: The praying parent as evangelist

Becky, a 21-year-old college student, had grown up knowing that her dad attended church services regularly. What she didn't know was that he began most days by praying and reading his Bible at 5:30 in the morning before heading off to work. One day Becky got up early to prepare for a college exam. She discovered her dad at the kitchen table reading his Bible. She was greatly surprised, although she had wondered why the Bible always rested on top of the microwave. Now she knew, and the moment touched her life in ways that her dad's routine attendance at worship services had not. The Christian faith gained new vitality for her as she witnessed in her dad a commitment to living and growing in his faith in a way she had never known before. In that early-morning discovery, two worlds were bridged. Later, as she reflected on that moment in a college course exploring the connection between church and culture she concluded, "I think I'm going back to church."

Lily Pad Roots: Bridging the gap

These two spiritual worldviews need to be brought closer together. The world of church traditions and historic Christian theology needs to be linked more consciously with the world of a personal spirituality that seeks something to believe in. This world must also integrate the whole of one's life with that which seems real and meaningful to individuals and communities. The second world needs an encounter with the specificity of the Christian faith, the domain of the first world. The first world experiences the challenge of an all-too-comfortable church tradition. Similarly, the second world has difficulty grasping the Christian faith in a way that appears dictated by church hierarchies and guided by a church tradition that most people have never known or have long forgotten. To one degree or another, most people reading this book live in both these worlds. The two worlds need not be distinct and opposing camps. Both reflect the Christian faith and presence of the Holy Spirit. Linking these two worlds is not a new quest, but one that needs ongoing, and perhaps renewed, attention today.

In the early church, the bridge between the publicly gathered community of Christians with all its Christian rhetoric and institutional structure and the personal expression of the faith with all the concomitant longings and uncertainties was baptism. Whereas today nearly anyone can walk into congregational worship services and fully participate in the service—sometimes even the Lord's Supper—in the early church, it was quite different. Evidence exists from the instructional writings of the second to the fifth century that a clear divide existed between the two. Those who had not been baptized had to leave the worship service prior to the praying of the Lord's Prayer and the celebration of the Lord's Supper. Persons desiring to become Christian had to be baptized before fully participating in the life of the church.

To be baptized in the early church was to be allowed into the full mystery of Christian worship through the public praying of the Lord's Prayer and eating the Lord's meal. (Both baptism and the Lord's Supper were referred to as "the mysteries.") Prior to one's baptism (specifically adult baptism), those who desired to be a part of the community (catechumens) were taught the good news of Jesus Christ, and were mentored in the practice of the faith. At the time of baptism, the catechumen not only publicly confessed the Christian faith in the presence of other Christians, but a mentor also attested to the life of that individual. The catechumen was to have already been practicing the faith through such acts as caring for orphans and widows and regular participation in the worshiping community. The catechumen's life was publicly examined by these standards of Christian living. The person standing before the Christian gathering seeking baptism was, in essence, being asked, "Do you practice?"

When a person was baptized in the early church, one of the rituals was to remove his or her clothing, enter into the baptismal waters naked, and emerge from the waters to be clothed in a white garment signifying new birth and life in Christ:

> You were taught to put away your former way of life, your old self, corrupt and deluded by its lusts, and to be renewed in the spirit of your minds, and to clothe yourselves with the new self, created according to the likeness of God in true righteousness and holiness (Ephesians 4:22-24).

Colossians 2:12 speaks of being "buried with [Christ] in baptism," and being "raised with him through faith . . ." Colossians 3:5 goes on to exhort a new way of life: "Put to death, therefore, whatever in you is earthly: fornication, impurity, passion, evil desire, and greed (which is idolatry)." The letter continues with a positive exhortation of the baptized life when it states, "As God's chosen ones, holy and beloved, clothe yourselves with compassion, kindness, humility, meekness, and patience" (3:12).

Lily Pad Roots: Nothing new

During the Reformation, numerous leaders and movements sought to lift up the role of the home in the Christian faith. Parents, guardians, and others who had responsibility for the lives of children had the fundamental task of raising them in the Christian faith. The spiritual life of the Christian home that Martin Luther, John Calvin, Menno Simons, and others promoted and modeled within their own lives is a powerful legacy of the Reformation. For some of these leaders, baptism shaped the life of the home. Luther, for example, understood that baptism held the mystery to the "newness of life," the daily life in Christ. He taught that baptism is "so full of comfort and grace that heaven and earth cannot comprehend it."[2] He went on to affirm that in this sacrament "every Christian has enough to study and practice all his or her life."[3] Parents and others who served in the place of parents were the primary guides to the study and practice of baptism.

Recently, much emphasis has been placed on the remembrance of baptism in the lives of believers. When people hear the exhortation, "Remember your baptism," they often assume a simple mental exercise of recalling one's baptism on a certain date in history. But the baptismal life is more than a cognitive exercise of remembrance. The biblical concept of remembrance also included participation in the past event. Thus, the seder meal is a way for all generations of Jews to participate in the saving work of God in the exodus from Egypt. Further, at the Last Supper of Jesus with his disciples before his crucifixion, he said, "Do this in remembrance of me." To remember Jesus' Last Supper is also to participate in the saving work of God through Christ.

This is the sense of remembrance needed when one is exhorted to remember one's baptism. It signifies a participation in the saving work of God now and for all time. Luther refers to Romans 6:4 when he describes the daily life in Christ established in baptism. In the Small Catechism, Luther asks the question, "What does such baptizing with water signify?" He wrote,

> It signifies that daily the old person in us with all our sins and evil desires is to be drowned through sorrow for sin and repentance, and that daily a new person is to come forth and rise up to live before God in righteousness and purity forever.[4]

The life of baptism that one studies and practices in daily life forms the foundation for the Christian life in both the public and domestic spheres.

Baptism signifies a way of life that not only regularly confesses the Christian faith in words, but also in one's conduct, which includes loving acts of kindness as well as confession of sins and the pursuit of daily renewal through the forgiving grace of God. For Christian communities that regularly speak of baptism in the corporate life, an odd silence has arisen regarding the language of practice—of putting off the old self and putting on the garment of Christ through such things as compassion, kindness, humility, meekness, and patience.

Giving attention to the shape of the Christian life is not new. The life made holy by God's grace is central to the biblical message. It has been a regular topic for the hymns of the church and material for classic Christian writings like *The Confessions of St. Augustine*, *The Rule of St. Benedict*, *The Imitation of Christ* by Thomas à Kempis, *The Spiritual Exercises of St. Ignatius*, John Bunyan's *Pilgrim's Progress*, Philip Jacob Spener's *Pia Desideria*, and Dietrich Bonhoeffer's *Life Together*. What seems needed today, in a culture that lifts up as the norm a privatized sense of spirituality and a home life that has lost its spiritual anchor, is help in identifying a Christian life for the home. The goal of the Four Keys is to help households express and explore a common Christian faith in a way that supports, challenges, and informs all in the home who claim—or want to claim—the Christian faith as their ultimate source of strength, hope, and love.

Lily Pad Roots: Risky business

Christian practice involves risk and the potential for misuse, and promoting the salutary effects of the Four Keys in the life of congregations and homes is no exception. Congregational life, by its very nature, is messy, as is family life. The Scriptures indicate that the life of faith is messy, too. In Genesis, for example, Jacob wrestles with God and is given a new name: Israel. Time and again the kings of Israel and Judah are put to the test and often come up short, turning to other gods or other nations for guidance or salvation. The prophet Hosea marries the prostitute Gomer, symbolizing the unfaithfulness of God's people. God's prophetic word condemns the people and uncovers their shame. It appears that they would be abandoned, but instead they were to be brought out to the wilderness where God would tenderly woo the people back (see Hosea 2:6-15).

The waters of faith are rough in the New Testament as well. Instead of displaying exemplary faith, Jesus' disciples often act out of ignorance and disbelief, demonstrating time and again that Christian faith is about God's grace rather than human achievement. The baptismal life of discipleship conveys a vital, life-and-death, all-or-nothing side that reflects God's will at work in the lives of followers. The New Testament focus on baptism in one's daily life is nowhere more clearly stated than in Romans 6:

> Do you not know that all of us who have been baptized into Christ Jesus were baptized into his death? Therefore we have been buried with him by baptism into death, so that, just as Christ was raised from the dead by the glory of the Father, so we too might walk in newness of life (Romans 6:3-4).

The apostle Paul describes baptism through the imagery of death and resurrection. Because of the grace of God given in baptism, Paul exhorts Christians to "present [themselves] to God as those who have been brought from death to life" (Romans 6:13). Birth, death, and resurrection are mysterious moments that are epiphanies of the divine, and baptism is the key that opens the believer to a blessed and vulnerable life of faith.

We now turn our attention to a detailed discussion of the Four Keys: caring conversation; a devotional life that is both public and domestic; service; and rituals and traditions. They present a way for the Christian to die to the old sinful self and be open to the new that only God can birth.

NOTES

1. Peter L. Benson and Carolyn H. Eklin, *Effective Christian Education: A Summary Report on Faith, Loyalty, and Congregational Life* (Minneapolis: Search Institute, 1990), p. 38.
2. *The Book of Concord, Martin Luther's Large Catechism,* Robert Kolb and Timothy J. Wengert, eds. (Minneapolis: Fortress Press, 2000), 461.
3. Ibid., 461.
4. *A Contemporary Translation of Luther's Small Catechism,* Timothy J. Wengert, trans. (Minneapolis: Augsburg Fortress, 1994), 43.

CHAPTER NINE

Croaking Frogs,
Key 1—Caring conversations

After a lecture on nurturing faith in the home and congregation to a group of theology students and faculty at the University of Lund (Sweden) School of Divinity, a question concerning the methodological principles and pedagogical approach to nurturing the Christian faith was asked. (This kind of question is often not asked in workshop settings, but since the dialogue took place at a divinity school, it is not surprising that it was asked.) After a pause to think about the question, the answer became clear: Our methodological principle and pedagogical approach are relationship and story.

The Christian faith is transmitted from generation to generation through personal, trusted relationships that share the stories of the family, the faith, and the Bible. The Holy Spirit works through these relationships, stories, and the conversations that give substance to them, blessing the recipient with the gift of faith. The conversations in which we engage—that is, the stories of our lives that we share with others—reveal volumes about the faith and values that we hold dear. These conversations also shape the behavior and interests of our lives. The conversations and stories that happen among family, friends, and other valued people linger long after the actual conversation has been archived in our minds. These memories are also the vehicle of the Holy Spirit to edify the message and life of the gospel.

Caring conversations include more than simply telling our stories. At the heart of the communication recommended here is the sharing of faith, values, and the care of others. This can range from supportive listening, sharing the good news of Jesus Christ with another, and simple praise and thanksgiving to challenging admonition, ethical discussions, and a call to action on behalf of all God's creatures and creation. Whether it be helping another through a difficult decision, responding to global climatic changes and genetic engineering, or encouraging another in the midst of doubt regarding the Christian faith, the goal is to engage in dialogue that reflects the ministry of reconciliation that Christ brings to the world. Ours is a ministry of reconciliation that includes all forms of communication (see 2 Corinthians 5:18). This does not always mean the explicit naming of Jesus in each and every conversation, but it does mean that the life and salvation present through Jesus is in one's perspective. Although conversation through stories may not always be the most direct or helpful form of communication, it is our conviction that the sharing of stories often helps communicate and our own stories are almost always a part of the background for our convictions and conversations. The story of Jesus and our life stories are woven together as one fabric that brings forth endless variety of caring conversation.

Lily Pad Roots: "Keep the faith, baby!"

When people converse, the possibility always exists that the words may linger in the memories of those involved in the conversation. Words in meaningful conversations, can come back to speak again and again. That seems to be the point of Proverbs 6:20-22 referenced earlier:

> My child, keep your father's commandment, and do not forsake your mother's teaching. Bind them upon your heart always; tie them around your neck. When you walk, they will lead you; when you lie down, they will watch over you; and when you awake, they will talk with you.

This text is reminiscent of a cliché from the 60s: "Keep the faith, baby." Often spoken while passing or as a word of departure, the phrase served as encouragement to the hearer. "Keep the faith, baby" was almost a form of blessing that encouraged the recipient to stay committed and hopeful, and served as a reminder for daily renewal and daily practice. Many clichés have a similar intention: "Hang in there"; "Just do it!"; "No fear!"; "Carpe diem"; and "Peace out, dawg." They act as more than social exchange; they function as caring conversation and encouragement to live life truly and boldly. They are lingering words that stay with us throughout the day. "Keep the faith, baby" infers a context for lives and a relationship with otherness, perhaps even God (although this meaning was most likely not the original intent of the words).

The Proverbs text emphasizes the instruction of children through the teaching of the commandments and history of God's people. Through this teaching technique, the memory of the instructive words of parents speaks to the children (". . . they will talk with you . . ." (Proverbs 6:22). The words linger in the minds of the children and initiate an internal conversation. Clearly, adults are encouraged to have the kind of meaningful conversation with their children that will serve the children as a compass, a guide, and a protector along life's way. Such words of wisdom from parents and other caregivers carry divine power to renew and change lives.

The fundamental message of Proverbs 6 is simple: the teachings of the faith intimately connect with daily life. The words of mothers, fathers, and other caregivers impact the lives of children as they go their way and as they begin and end their daily routines. The importance of this point is as important for Christians as it was for the ancestors in the faith. It is difficult to imagine sharing and nurturing the message of Jesus Christ, especially with children and youth, without attention to daily living and personal conversation. People need more than the "correct" religion or doctrine. People need to know that the God in whom they place their trust truly cares about their lives. Recent research has demonstrated that homes in which faith conversation is engaged are more effective in nurturing the Christian faith in the lives of children. Such interaction influences the lives of children even when parents and other mentoring figures are not physically present.

Tadpole Tale: Parents' words have a way of sticking around

At the funeral of his father, a grieving son remembered life with his dad. Memories of times of talking and arguing together, of fishing and hunting trips, of stresses in the family, and moments of love and reconciliation flooded over him. Like many fathers of his generation, this man had invested himself in career and work as a sign of familial love. However, the result of this focus was absence from the family and vocational distractions when with the family, which were also etched in his son's memory. He said, "My dad taught me one thing I'll never forget: 'The only thing you have in life that's of any real value is your good name. Protect it.' I don't remember a lot of other things he said, but I remember that. It's pretty much my code of honor, my motto for life."

We all remember words our parents spoke that we carry with us. Hopefully, they are words that function as a "motto for life," but sometimes they are hurtful words. A talented and acclaimed singer remembers overhearing his father say to his mother, "Our son isn't going to amount to much of anything. He's worthless." These words scarred the singer and crippled him throughout his life. He was never able to achieve the success his voice offered. He had the talent, but his father's words that he carried with him were destructive. He lived his life fulfilling the prophecy of these words.

Lily Pad Roots: Mutual conversation and consolation

The fundamental quest for God through human conversation is historically as well as biblically rooted. In the Smalcald Articles written in 1537, Martin Luther identified the "mutual conversation and consolation" of the saints as a way the gospel extends God's "guidance and help" to people's lives.[1] Luther believed that such conversations had the power of the Spirit to heal people's lives through another person's "living voice."[2] The loneliness humans sometimes feel cannot adequately be overcome by voicemail or Internet messages. In the midst of the busyness of life, there is nothing like having a person stop in their tracks to speak and listen to us as individual creatures worthy of attention. That all-too-rare encounter has the power to heal lonely souls.

Luther identifies human experience as a divine balm that transcends time. He is very specific about using the language of faith in conversation, including the language of faith located in the catechism—the historic catechism of the church, not primarily Luther's Small Catechism—which is not only to be read and studied but shared in conversation. In such human dialogue "the Holy Spirit is present and bestows ever new and greater light and devotion, so that [the catechism] tastes better and better, and is digested . . ."[3] The historic catechism—that is, the Lord's Prayer, the Ten Commandments, and the Apostles' Creed—provides language, images, and ways of thinking and acting shaped by the Scriptures. The intent of the catechism is to impact the conversation and actions of Christians. For the Christian, the catechism is a natural application of Proverbs 6. The words of the catechism are not the sum of what is passed on to children, but they serve as a solid foundation of words that guide, protect, and speak faith to children.

Catechisms used by Roman Catholics, Episcopalians, Methodists, Presbyterians, Lutherans, and others to instruct children and youth with standardized and approved texts are, at best, intended to facilitate conversation in the home. The words of these texts can shape the language, interests, behavior, and consciousness of people. Even denominations that shy away from written catechisms often have well-developed "oral catechisms" that can work to instruct and indoctrinate persons in a particular understanding of the faith. Often these catechisms, either written or oral, have been reduced to function as instruments of indoctrination into a particular religious worldview that is usually removed from the day-to-day lives of the learners.

A Christian catechism—written or oral—has the potential to enrich conversations and reflect the vitality of the Christian message for daily life. A catechism can help people express themselves in their Christian witness whether in a home, congregation, school, workplace, or other setting. Conversations linked to specific Christian rhetoric are not intended to intimidate others or give the impression that all of life's questions have simple answers. They are a means to communicate in a unique moment in time. These conversations exhibit a search for understanding that stretches personal horizons and is grounded in the good news of Jesus Christ.

Tadpole Tales: A trip to the mall ends up at a thrift shop

When David's daughter, Kirsten, was in the seventh grade she loved to go to the mall and shop. At one point she wanted a particular pair of brand-name cut-off jeans. Her parents strongly urged Kirsten to buy a pair of jeans without the popular label. They were willing to pick up the $20 price tag, but would not pay $50 for the jeans she wanted. They expressed their concerns that she make good choices, practice good Christian stewardship, and avoid coveting and being consumed by possessions (the Ninth and Tenth Commandments).

Kirsten decided to pay the $30 difference out of her babysitting money. Dad was willing to take her to the mall to get her favorite cutoffs, but first he asked that they begin with a devotion (the second of the Four Keys) on Psalm 23:1, which he did not even bother to recite. He could see his daughter's mental wheels turning as she recited to herself, "The LORD is my shepherd, I shall not want." Once she got it, she rolled her eyes in that gesture that communicated, "Oh, Dad, you are so weird . . . and annoying." The two then went to purchase her jeans.

Weeks later Kirsten's mom, Gloria, noticed that she had not seen the jeans on Kirsten for some time. The subject came up when the three of them were on an afternoon walk through the neighborhood. Kirsten responded that the jeans had been stolen while on a service group activity at the local zoo. She was sure she knew who had the jeans, but she could not prove it. It was an irritating but memorable event in her life. After that, Kirsten decided on her own that cheaper jeans were just fine. In fact, as she got older, she preferred to buy her jeans and many other clothing items as thrift shops for sometimes as cheap as one dollar. Parental conversations (and Psalm 23) had all been part of a young woman's ethical development. Conversations, the sense of the divine in life, and a disappointing experience had intersected to create a character-forming moment in the life of a child.

Tadpole Tales: Where is the holy ground?

Caring conversation indicates an interest in others—their hurts, their joys, their concerns and dreams, their needs and wants, their values and faith. Jesus exhibits such conversational style when he meets people in homes, on the road on his journeys, or when questioning or being questioned by religious leaders.

A delightful exercise to do with adults, youth, or in a cross-generational group is to ask, "Where is the holy ground of your lives?" that is, "Where do you have those conversations where memorable, intimate dialogue takes place—conversation that conveys the peace, hope, and faith that God gives to your life?" The answers vary, but many are common from group to group: in the car, at the dinner table, tucking a child into bed, while doing chores, or while on vacation. The language of "holy ground" implies a recognized religious site that people routinely visit—churches, shrines, temples, mosques, and so on. But, when people reflect on their own life stories, they realize that their *lives* are holy ground. This has biblical precedent. Moses, for example, encountered God in a burning bush far from recognized religious sites while tending to his daily work.

An exercise such as the one described above helps people identify how God has blessed their lives with the precious ground of caring conversation. It is important for people not only to name these occasions but also to claim these times and places as their own and as a particular gift from God.

Finally, because it is precious, memorable, God-given ground, people need to find their way back to it. It is not enough for people to claim and name their holy ground; they need to find their way back to this holy ground again and again. People need a road map to help them remember how they got there in the past and figure out how to return in the future. It is not uncommon for people to remember and long for wonderful family occasions that fostered memorable conversations, but the road map that got them there has been lost as the family travels the highway of busy schedules and numerous obligations.

We (the authors) regularly tucked our children into bed when they were little, but let go of that routine as they grew. Jeremy helped his dad get back to that routine a number of years ago. One night, after long committee meetings in the congregation, dad came home bone tired and plopped down in his favorite chair. He thought everyone was asleep, but from a distance he heard his son's familiar voice calling out, "Isn't someone going to lie down with me?" What an opportunity to be reminded of how important that moment is, no matter what the age of the child. The memory of Jeremy's voice and pleading question has served as a treasured roadmap kept for constant reference, and through such mental recall, dad found his way back again and again to the holy ground of parent-child conversation.

Holy ground can easily be lost. Most families remember those times and locations in their lives that are no longer visited. Many family members might say, "We used to do that. Why don't we do that anymore?" Constant vigilance is needed to keep households connected to the holy ground of their lives. Congregations attentive to the importance of such conversational space can do much to help families identify the importance of such space and can help them revisit these places to facilitate meaningful, caring conversation.

Tadpole Tale: A golden necklace

Not only is it valuable to name, claim, and find one's way back to the holy ground of precious, caring conversation, it is also important to pursue new opportunities for meaningful contact. One of our favorite stories exemplifies this point. A young woman was about to enter high school. Her parents were both excited and concerned about this milestone event in her life. They were excited for many new experiences for growth that would take place. These parents remembered their own high school years with great delight. But at the same time, they were concerned about the potential for peer pressure and the temptation to make choices that could be harmful to their daughter's present and future life—temptations such as drugs, sexual activity, alcohol consumption, and so on. It was not that their daughter had acted irresponsibly in the past. The parents understood that these years would be both exciting and challenging, and they had concerns about the power of certain peer-group influences.

On behalf of both parents, Mom took the daughter out to dinner to celebrate this milestone and to talk about the challenges ahead. She expressed her value of virginity before marriage and hoped the daughter would want that for herself. The daughter acknowledged that it was the way she wanted to live her life, too. At the end of the meal, Mom gave the daughter a simple gold necklace. She said to her daughter that whenever she wore it, saw it on her dresser, or just thought about it, she was to remember that her parents were praying for her through her high school years, and for her commitment to make wise, safe, and faithful choices.

The mother then said a little prayer for both of them while they sat there at the restaurant. After the prayer, the mother looked up to see her daughter was crying. The first thought the mother had was that she had done something wrong; she had gone too far (an understandable response in a society that is not very supportive of parents or parenting). But she mustered the courage to ask her daughter what was wrong. The daughter simply said, "Mom, you've never done anything like this for me before." During that special mother-daughter occasion, new holy ground had been found.

Lily Pad Roots: Teens want adults who listen

The daughter's response is consistent with other youth her age who want more time for meaningful conversations with parents. Youth will often not give parents clear clues that they want to talk, but surveys over the years have shown an interest on the part of youth in *cross*-generational conversation in the home. The trappings of the teenage world have simply created so many obstacles to candid self-disclosure that the desire for parent-teen conversation has often been missed. Between the cell phone conversations from behind closed bedroom doors, bedroom televisions, bedroom computers, instant messaging, chat room conversations, e-mail correspondence, and busy schedules, it is easy to understand how the generations pass like ships in the night as youth and adults enter and leave the home, and how a teenager could respond to holy ground conversation with the words, "Mom (Dad), you have never done anything like this for me before."

Over the years, we have been asking teenagers the same question, "What is it that you want from the adults around you?" The response is nearly always the same: "We want them to listen to us." This seems so simple, doesn't it? Our ears are critical tools for passing on the faith. From the adult perspective, caring conversation mostly involves listening and being available. Often this listening is done around the dinner table, and in fact, research has shown that one of the few common denominators found among National Merit Scholars is that they tended to come from families that ate dinner together. Much caring conversation takes place around the dinner table. Jesus certainly understood this. His ministry was built, in part, around eating with others, whether it was feeding 5,000, dinner with Zacchaeus, or eating in the home of Mary and Martha.

More homes need life-affirming parent-child conversations today. For example, over 90 percent of the sexual activity either alluded to or engaged in on prime-time television is between singles. Clearly, parental silence regarding sexual values, moral conduct, and healthy, life-affirming choices is not helpful. While it is an accepted norm that couples live together before marriage, an abundance of research exists that shows this norm is not helpful to healthy, enduring relationships. But unless parents, pastors, and other mentors of faith, values, and character formation speak up, youth will be left in the hands of a consumer-based culture that is more interested in their pocketbooks than their relationships.

Youth are, in fact, waiting to hear what parents and other mentors and caregivers think and value, even if the youth do not always demonstrate their interest and curiosity about such things. Throughout the teenage years, parents are the primary influence on youth in terms of values, faith, and long-term choices. Parents need not abdicate this role out of fear and frustration that peers have all the power. It just isn't so. But without opportunities for caring conversation, parents will not likely find out otherwise. The primary challenge for parents is to speak to their children and youth. Perhaps they may not say things correctly, but silence may be a worse option.

Consider the power of the media upon our children. In 1950, at the dawn of the era of television, only 170 youth below the age of 15 *nationwide* were arrested for serious crimes such as rape, murder, aggravated assault, or robbery! This number increased by *11,000 percent* by 1979.[4] Of course, it is difficult to make direct cause-and-effect relationships between watching television and social behavior, but the impact of the one on the other seems irrefutable. A consumer-based society, with its highly sophisticated advertising industry that relies upon television and other media to influence potential customers, has a goal of creating product loyalty by age three. For some products it is earlier than that.[5] Parental silence regarding values that are very different from those of a consumer-based society that uses sex and violence to promote product loyalty is devastating. The need for caring conversations between children and parents (and other adult caregivers) to affirm the lives of children and help shape their values and faith is imperative.

Tadpole Tale: Beefcake

When Paul's son Josh was 15, he and his dad observed that they didn't have much in common. Josh liked choir and martial arts. Dad was into work, sports, and outdoor activities. They weren't doing anything together. Josh, however, kept saying he wanted to fix up a truck. That sounded interesting to dad, too, so they bought an ancient, one-ton pickup. The body, painted primer gray, seemed a lost cause, but it had a huge V8 engine and a four-barrel carburetor that swallowed gasoline like a Little Leaguer drinking a juice box on a 90-degree day.

It was love at first sight for Josh and his dad. These were not the emotions of the women of the home. The day Dad drove this beast home, dubbed *Beefcake* by Josh, mom took one look at it, rolled her eyes and said, "This eludes me." She walked into the house and would have no more to do with *Beefcake*, and Josh's sister refused to ride in it. Josh and his dad, on the other hand, were having a superb male bonding experience Josh and his dad plunged eagerly into this project, despite the fact that neither of them exhibited mechanical skill. They soon discovered that it is possible for oil to leak from just about anywhere. They also learned that they could fix the leaks. The highlight of their time with *Beefcake* was when they put glass-packs on the exhaust system. (Glass-packs are a light-duty muffler designed to create a maximum amount of noise at the tailpipe end. With this engine, they could drown out a whole herd of Harleys.) They worked all Friday evening, finally completing the task around 11:00. Since there were now two teenagers working on this project (dad had seriously regressed), they had to start it up and see how it sounded. Remember, it was 11:00 P.M. in a quiet residential neighborhood. The sound was a symphony of cylinders, combustion, and power. They took off down the street revving the engine with each gearshift. At one point in their late night traveling Josh turned to his dad and said, "Dad, this is the coolest thing you have ever done." Dad almost wept for joy, but hit Josh in the arm instead.

Unfortunately, fixing *Beefcake* became more expensive and time consuming than either of them could commit to, so they gave the truck to a camp. The bonds from their *Beefcake* experience live on, however. Nearly every time dad is with Josh, who has since left home for college, the conversation eventually drifts back to their *Beefcake* experience. They laugh, relive moments, exaggerate, and talk. This is caring conversation. It anchors the relationship in ways Josh and dad could not have imagined. Dad will admit that they didn't talk much about the faith during those *Beefcake* times. However, both Josh and dad are convinced that if Jesus were around today, he'd drive a pickup rather than a donkey, and both confess that their current conversations of faith are deeply rooted in the mutual experience of a big V8 with glass-packs.

Lily Pad Roots: Gender differences
Caring conversation looks different between males and females.[7] In general, boys do not develop verbal skills as quickly as girls. Boys often need help in developing verbal skills, especially in identifying and naming emotions.

The male brain functions differently from that of females. Boys use more of the right side of their brain while girls use both sides more equally, perhaps because girls have a larger *corpus callosum* (that part of the brain that connects the two spheres). The right side of the brain is designed for spatial processing rather than reading, emoting, and verbal processing. Not surprisingly, boys generally have less developed reading skills than their female counterparts of the same age. As a result, boys engage in caring conversation through action (like fixing a truck) or problem-solving rather than sitting and talking.[8]

Second, boys begin to pull away from their mothers around the age of eight or nine while generally speaking girls do this much later. It's not unusual for a mother to be hurt by this experience. She'll seek caring conversation and want to hug her "little boy" and he'll stiffen up or squirm away from her and this form of affection. Her son is trying to explore and manipulate his space through such means as building forts, taking things apart, or riding his bike. His agenda has changed, in part, from being anchored to mom to moving out into the world. He still remains anchored by mom, but the relationship has changed and affection is expressed differently. Mothers can be reassured in the knowledge that boys who begin this outward movement navigate it best when they have a good, solid relationship with their mother. This relationship gives them the confidence and reassurance they need. At this time, it is also crucial that a boy have another significant male with whom to bond. This could be the boy's father, a coach, a teacher, a mentor, a pastor, a scout leader, or a trusted neighbor. The boy benefits from a man in his life in order for caring conversation to take place in developmentally effective ways.

A third distinction regarding boys and caring conversation relates to how they bond. Whereas girls generally bond through intimacy and sharing, boys will often bond through competition, acts of personal sacrifice, commitment to a mission (for example, sports), or an adventure. The point is, caring conversation can look quite different depending upon the gender of a child. Adults who care for youth and congregational leaders need to avoid the "one size fits all" approach to caring conversation as a part of nurturing the faith of children and youth.

Tadpole Tale: The wrestling mat as holy ground

The distinction in bonding behavior between boys and girls can be baffling to female adults working with boys. A male advisor helped develop an after-school program for area junior high youth. The program is held in a local church in the community. In the early phase of development, the predominantly female staff was quite distressed by the behavior of the junior high boys. After a full day of school the boys would roll into the church, make lots of noise, and wrestle and tussle with one another.

One of the female staff noted, "I don't know what to do with the boys" (meaning: "They are rough, rowdy, and threatening to me"). The male advisor, upon observing the exact same phenomenon, asked, "So what's the problem?" (meaning: "They are acting like boys fresh out of school needing to blow off some steam"). As the conversation developed it became apparent that the female leaders had a "female understanding" of how boys are to behave in an after-school program: they wanted the boys to sit down and "tell them about their day." This works for some boys, but many won't open up in this way.

Recognizing that boys will bond and communicate differently, the program purchased some wrestling mats and laid them out for the boys. The rule was that they could come in and tussle and wrestle like lion cubs as long as they started from their knees and an adult male was supervising. It worked wonderfully. The male advisor often supervises this "boy time," and either as a group or one at a time, they often stop, talk, and ask questions of the advisor and share their day. Then they return again to their mats for group bonding, friendly competition, and exercise. The wrestling mats are holy ground.

Congregations wishing to have caring conversation with boys need to recognize that they generally operate out of a female model of communication. Not surprisingly, boys feel alienated in church and are leaving in droves. We do a disservice to the way God has made boys by expecting them to conform to a "one size fits all" method of communication and community building. Congregations are asking them to deny their very nature in this way. We often joke, but with some serious intent, that a boy-friendly congregation would have a gym and a car hoist. These two "boy magnets" would go a long way in addressing male methods of communicating.

Recently, junior high report cards came out. While the boys in the after-school program wrestled they voluntarily lined up to present their grades to the male advisor, who was stunned by their willingness to share. Some of the grades he saw would not be worth bragging about. Nevertheless he went through each report card with the boys and then asked each of them a significant question: "Which of the scores were they going to pull up by one full letter grade?" Each decided which grade had to be improved, and the goal was set. What was the incentive for the boys to go through such an exercise? The after-school program had utilized a high elements challenge course where the boys could climb and test their skills and courage. They loved this activity. The advisor promised to take them to the course again when the grades came up. Caring conversation for boys often looks like this. When boys sense a caring man in their life, are given opportunity to be who God made them to be, and are challenged in a positive community atmosphere, boys will thrive.

Lily Pad Roots: The need for time

Reflective and attentive conversations have the potential to influence the lifestyle, character, faith, and values of youth. Most families today need the active support of the church to name, claim, and find roadmaps to the holy ground of life-affirming conversations. This process of finding the roadmap and enjoying the discovery of personal conversation takes time.

Time is a precious commodity in our schedule-stressed lives. Two types of time exist: urgent time and essential time. Urgent time screams at us, telling us we are late, not ready, and certainly not good enough to deal with the daily demands of life. Essential time whispers to us, asking questions like "Have you taken time for a friend, family member, or stranger?", "Have you taken time for yourself?" or, "Have you taken time for prayer, Scripture reading, or meditation on the wonder of life?" Urgent time is born of guilt, condemnation, and fear. It typically offers the first prayer of the day, one that may be expressed before getting out of bed in the morning: "Oh, my God, I'm late!" It doesn't matter if you get up on time or not. You still have this gnawing sensation that all is not well and that you needed more time to prepare for the day. Urgent time shows no mercy.

The church, the chosen people of God, has been given the mystery of God's will—"a plan for the fullness of time, to gather up all things in him, things in heaven and things on earth" (Ephesians 1:10). Christians have been blessed with every spiritual blessing, and were chosen before time began (see Ephesians 1:3-4). Christians know of things that are beyond the urgent and that plumb the depths of what is truly essential. The urgent demands of life can be like the man who built bigger barns to store more crops for future benefits, but did not know that his life had come to an end. He did not understand the true needs of the moment (see Luke 12:21).

In the midst of building bigger barns, sometimes life itself is lost. The danger of urgent time—be it time to invest in more fortuitous stocks, to buy fancier cars, to go on more exotic vacations, or time to achieve greater things than one's peers—is to miss the mark of God's gift of time. Even the people in our own homes and our most precious relationships are overlooked as we pursue what seems so urgent and necessary. The screams of urgent time can make us deaf to rich opportunities around us for moments of caring, sharing, and building up the body of Christ, and serving the needs of the world in faith, hope, and love.

The church resists speaking out about the spiritual dimension of time, and that is sad. A restaurant chain offering take-out meals can promote the value of family time for dinner at home through television adds, but the church that promotes family dinner time for the sake of faith, values, and character formation is judged as naïve and insensitive to busy people. It seems acceptable to promote family dinners for profit, but not for health and faith. And yet, the evidence is clear—time, essential time, is needed to strengthen family relationships and to pass on faith and values between the generations.

How we use time says a lot about what god(s) we trust. When we confess our own sins, at the core of our lives lingers a latent polytheism. The most grievous sin is turning to false gods—the gods of comfort and safety, the gods of acclaim and superiority, the gods of self-sufficiency and self-worship, the god of being the one who has to be right in the presence of family, friend, or stranger. So much about our broken lives leads us away from the quintessential prayer and expression of faith that comes from Mary the mother of Jesus: "Let it be to me according to your word" (Luke 1:38). So much about our broken lives leads us away from taking the time, essential time, to care for others through attentive eyes, ears, and voices.

According to psychologist Michael Gurian, the average adult in America today works more hours a year than an adult did in previous decades, therefore taking more time away from family and children.[9] The *National Longitudinal Study of Adolescent Health* reports that in 1998 the average teenager in America spent 10 to 12 less hours with his/her parents each week than in 1960 (see www.cpc.unc.edu/addhealth). That is a minimum of 520 hours of lost caring conversation time. How we use our time is a spiritual issue. As with our checkbooks, the way we use time reflects our priorities in life. How parents use their time is a basic issue to be addressed in Christian parenting.

In our travels to other cultures we are always impressed by the amount of time people spend together. For example, in Guyana, South America, most evenings are spent talking outside in public places or on front porches with no purpose other than to gather. This is relaxed, spontaneous, cross-generational, and fun. Sadly, as satellite dishes begin to appear in the urban areas of Guyana, WWF wrestling and reruns of *I Love Lucy* are replacing this tradition. A number of community leaders in Guyana expressed their concerns regarding the "lawlessness" taking over their society. They were not talking about crime so much as moral deterioration. In their minds, moral deterioration was directly related to the outside cultural influences of the global media and the reconfiguration of time. Time for the family, the clan, or the community was being eaten up by a new value system bent on an individualistic use of time for work or entertainment.

Caring conversation is a key to nurturing faith in the home, and caring conversation requires time. Here, the congregation has a calling and a responsibility to encourage households to take time to listen, to respond, and to edify one another for the ministry of the gospel and the encouragement of individual lives.

Lily Pad Roots: Quality and quantity of time

Promoting "quality time" is not enough. Children do not distinguish between quality and quantity time as adults do. This distinction, makes little sense to children. Caring conversation is not only about what you do together, but also about being in one another's presence. Often the occasions that adults select for "quality time" do not match the rhythm and timing of children and youth. Adults need to be available and ready for the unplanned moments when children explode with ideas, questions, and reflections. Often the Spirit works through these unforeseen moments as the occasions for meaningful and memorable conversations.

A particle accelerator is a huge circular tunnel (often miles in length) that scientists use to accelerate the speed of atoms. As these atoms travel faster and faster, nearly reaching the speed of light, they crash into one another and become even smaller atoms or bits of atomic structure. Scientists do these experiments to learn more about the nature of matter and the universe. Life in America today is like living in a particle accelerator. As we move faster and faster in our culture, time seems to get shorter and shorter; we speed, we rush, and we hurry. As a result, we become less attached to one another. We continue to atomize. When we do run into one another, it is only for a brief moment of time before we split off atomized, isolated, and individualized even more.

Life in the American particle accelerator has parents rushing children to events, soccer games, and music lessons. Teenagers start their day at 6:00 A.M., rush through school, rush through sports or other after school activities, rush through homework and meals, leaving precious little time for friends and even less for families. Adults spend hours in commutes or clogged on freeways where they sit alone, away from family and friends.

This is America today, full of talk radio but little communication. We have "real TV" rather than a real life with our children. Much sentiment is expressed but too little interaction takes place, especially with our children.

The goals sought in quality time are often not accomplished with the minimum amount of time that quality time suggests. Time is required that goes beyond that which can be programmed. The parent who has set aside 10 or 15 minutes of "quality time" to repair and nurture a child's day may be vastly disappointed. The very idea that a few minutes well spent can heal lives is an example of hearing the screaming agendas of life without attention to the whispering sounds of essentials. Indeed, quality time conveys an unrealistic expectation that scheduled time, especially that between parent and child, suffices. While it is good to plan for times to have one-on-one or larger group conversation, such times simply do not satisfy the need for meaningful conversations between friends and family. Memorable and valued conversations simply do not always happen "on demand." What works and is planned by an adult may not fit with the attention level, interest, or emotional readiness of a child. The moment the adult is ready to give attention to the child may not be the moment the child is ready to share with the adult. We speak of "teachable moments," but need to recognize "conversational moments," those times when both parent and child find themselves engaged in meaningful dialogue that has not been planned. These times happen in the car or after dinner or before bed—on occasions and in ways that surprise.

Tadpole Tale: Essential time

Three adult sisters joined their father at the hospital bedside of their dying mother. The mother had only a short time to live. Her breathing was labored and her skin was ashen. Two of the sisters could no longer watch. They retired to a family lounge down the hall. The third sister felt obligated to remain through these crucial moments. At one point, the daughter noticed that her mother's lips kept moving. She told her dad that she wished she knew what her mom was trying to say. Her dad responded, "Oh, that's easy. She's saying her prayers. Every night of our marriage your mother and I have said the same bedtime prayer. If you look closely you can see her saying it now." After a pause to be in sync with his wife he spoke with her, "Now I lay me down to sleep. I pray the Lord my soul to keep. If I should die before I wake, I pray the Lord my soul to take." The daughter had never known of her parents' bedtime prayer life until that moment. She will never forget that night on holy ground. Essential time for conversation at mealtime, bedtime, or any other time is a spiritual issue. The church in the home and in the congregation has a message to share that seeks nothing less than essential time for the care, edification, encouragement, and renewal of lives.

Lily Pad Roots: The need for scheduled time

Of course, routine, scheduled time for families and friendship groups to engage in conversation and sharing is important. Disciplined investment in time set aside to enjoy and be enriched by personal conversations is needed. Both planned and unplanned conversations foster healthy relationships and the passing on of faith, values, and character strengths.

The practice of having times and places set aside to give others undivided attention and to practice the art of conversation is a special gift. These can include parent-child trips to the park or a restaurant, a morning prayer breakfast, an evening gathering at a coffee house with friends, or a family meeting to plan activities and review the happenings of the past week and plan for the next one. All of these examples lift up the value of spending deliberate time together, listening, speaking, and being sensitive to the needs of one another and supporting one another's dreams and aspirations. Such occasions fill our lives with memories, stories, and thoughts about faith, values, and goals that become the material for unplanned moments for reflection.

As the apostle Paul observes in Galatians 3:7, those who have faith in Jesus Christ are descendants of Abraham. Paul's immediate reference is to the inheritance of the blessing, the promise of the good news through faith, which, received in faith, comes to people who have real stories of hopes and fears, love and hate, trust and jealousy, loyalty, trickery, and deceit to tell. To learn of the stories of Abraham and Sarah, Isaac and Rebecca, and Jacob with Leah and Rachel, and all their descendants within and beyond the Scriptures, is to learn something of the character, meaning, faith journey, and messiness of our own personal and family experiences.

Relating a biblical account to present circumstances offers a valuable commentary on current events, whether personal or communal. Our life stories need to be told and need an interpretive frame for the telling. For the Christian community, the Bible offers an essential contribution to that interpretive frame. The uncertainties of family life experienced today are no different from the fragile existence of people in the Scriptures. The biblical narrative covers the full gamut of human emotion and relational dynamics as today but in a different historical setting. The Bible includes accounts of unexpected joy, doubt, murder, adultery, exemplary faith, hope, despair, intrigue, sibling rivalry, marital discord, young and very sensual love. It is all held together by a fundamental claim on our lives by a loving, providential creator God who never gives up on humanity and the larger created order. Neither the reality of human sin nor the restoration of human dignity through Christ is minimized. The biblical story provides many expressions of and comparisons to the ups and downs of daily life experienced today. Caring conversation is a means by which these accounts and experiences are remembered and come alive in meaningful ways for us today.

Tadpole Tale: Post 9-11

We have already noted how caring conversation came to the forefront following the terrorist attacks of September 11, 2001. People refocused, reconnected, reestablished, or reinforced ties with friends and loved ones. Phone calls, e-mails, letters, and extended meals and coffee breaks took place all over America.

At one junior high school, clergy, counselors, teachers, and parent volunteers were brought together following the attacks to meet with students and listen to their concerns and address their questions. The last hour of the day was left open for any student to come to the school library and meet with this group of adults. "I don't really know how many students will come," commented the school's principal. "It could be five or it could be more." To everyone's surprise the room was filled with troubled, questioning, and nervous youth who sat around tables and talked. The big question, "Why would this happen?" was not easily answered, but who really has an answer to that question? The setting was created, however, where caring conversation could take place in the school.

Similar scenes and gatherings took place throughout the United States on that terrible day. Perhaps, for a moment, we came to realize that we need one another and we need to talk with one another. The issues of our busy lives took a backseat to matters of life and death. Sharing caring conversation with our children and youth was, is, and will continue to be a matter of life and death. This critical practice of living out the gospel must be a daily priority for us.

Croaks, Ribbits, and Hops
1. FAITHTALK

A challenge for today's church—both in the home and in the congregation—is to form people who know the biblical story and who can tell their own stories. Ultimately, the language and imagery of the biblical story needs to be a frame of reference and guide in the telling of personal stories. The stories of the Bible are the family stories of the people of faith that connect them to the descendants in the faith. The value of relationships and stories is essential to passing on the Christian faith, and promotes both biblical literacy and the art of storytelling.

One tool to facilitate planned conversational times is the use of *FaithTalk* cards developed through The Youth and Family Institute. *FaithTalk* cards are non-threatening conversation starters that help individuals share their life stories, personal commitments, values, and particular life-shaping moments. Try getting a set and using them in your family, youth groups, small groups, in the car on vacation trips, or in other ways that you can think of.

David's father, Maynard, for example, shared an important story in his life at a family dinner celebrating his grandson's graduation from high school. After the meal, *FaithTalk* cards were distributed around the table. Maynard's card asked him to share his earliest memory of attending a funeral. It happened to be his mother's funeral when he was a teenager living on a farm. The death occurred during a snowstorm that left so much snow on the ground that the family had difficulty getting to the church for the funeral. As Maynard told it, the surrounding community came to the family farm with their own farm equipment and dug them out so they could have the funeral service as planned. It was a significant story and memory from Maynard's life filled with life and death, love and grief, Christian worship and service, family life and community life. The family gathered around that dinner table was moved by a story they had never heard before.

2. PERSONAL NOTES

Individual schedules greatly impact the timing and method for caring conversations. Sometimes those meaningful conversations begin with a note on the bathroom mirror or an e-mail message. One father wanted to share something of himself with his high school daughter each morning before he went to work. Since he left home before she got out of bed, his options were limited. During her senior year of high school he began a practice of leaving his daughter a personal note that he would he would stick on her bedroom mirror. Each day she would rise to find what he had left for her. During the evenings and weekends the two had a little more to talk about. The messages from Dad were so valuable to her that she kept them all. Those little notes became all the more precious to her the following year when her dad died unexpectedly of a heart attack.

Consider making little notes for family or friends to let them know you are thinking of them and that you care.

3. E-MAIL

E-mail messages have become another way of communication between family members. One mother of a junior high son was frustrated that she couldn't have meaningful conversations with her son. She noticed that each day he would come home and immediately read and write e-mail messages, so she decided to start there. She communicated with him by e-mail, and to her surprise he responded with lengthy e-mail messages in return. To Mom's great delight, as a consequence of the e-mail correspondence, the two of them began to speak more regularly with one another.

4. FAMILY MEETINGS

Caring conversations need to be intentional and scheduled. Regular family meetings are one way to achieve this goal. The format needs to be consistent: same time, same place, and the same people. Toys, TVs, food, and other distractions must be set aside. Find a place that acts as holy ground for your family, such as the dinner table, the living room, or on the deck. The following is a suggested structure.

   a) Open with prayer.
   b) Share compliments with one another (every person must compliment every other person including himself or herself).
   c) Address agenda items (an agenda here is simply a list of issues that surface throughout the week. The refrigerator door is usually a good place to put such a list where anyone can write concerns).
   d) Do a family activity together, such as *FaithTalk* cards or a game.
   e) Do 30 minutes of family chores together (this is service, another of the Four Keys).
   f) Close with prayer.
   g) Bring out refreshments or a full meal.

Family meetings are not a place where marital grievances are aired, they are a place where support and communication is encouraged and practiced. Rotate the leadership for the meeting among all family members so that leadership skills can be developed.

Family meetings are effective with families, church youth groups, sports teams, church school classes, council meetings, and so on.

NOTES

1. *The Book of Concord,* Smalcald Articles, Robert Kolb and Timothy J. Wengert, eds. (Minneapolis: Fortress Press, 2000), 319.

2. *Luther's Letters of Spiritual Counsel,* Theodore Tappert, ed. and trans. (Philadelphia: Westminster Press, 1955), 101.

3. *The Book of Concord, Martin Luther's Large Catechism,* Robert Kolb and Timothy J. Wengert, eds. (Minneapolis: Fortress Press, 2000), 381.

4. *Selling Out America's Children* by David Walsh gives ample documentation on the use of media to sell products. (Minneapolis: Fairview Press, 1994.)

5. Miriam Miedzian, *Boys Will Be Boys* (New York: Anchor Books, 1988), 218.

7. Since boys and men tend to be less involved in the life of the church than girls and women, in the section that follows we will focus on male styles of communication and learning. For a more detailed look at the communication and learning styles of females, see *Boys and Girls Learn Differently* by Michael Gurian (San Francisco: Jossey-Bass, 2001), Mary Pipher, *Reviving Ophelia: Saving the Selves of Adolescent Girls* (New York: Ballentine Books, 1994), and Mary Stewart Van Leeuwen, *My Brother's Keeper: What the Social Sciences Do and Don't Tell Us About Masculinity* (Downer's Grove: Intervarsity Press, 2002).

8. William Pollack has written extensively on this subject in his book, *Real Boys: Rescuing our Sons from the Myths of Boyhood* (New York: Henry Holt and Company, 1998). See also *Boys and Girls Learn Differently* by Michael Gurian.

9. Michael Gurian, *The Wonder of Boys* (New York: Tarcher/Putnam, 1996).

CHAPTER TEN

Praying Church Frogs
Key 2—Devotions

The concept of individual or family devotions suggests a practice that takes place generally in and through the life of the home, but our understanding of the practice also includes the congregation. For many Christians, a life devoted to God's word is almost exclusively experienced in the congregation. It is not enough, however, to gather periodically in a public setting to receive God's grace through Word and Sacrament ministry. The Christian life is edified by God's word for a life of prayer, praise, and thanksgiving in both home and congregation, and the congregation has a major responsibility to model, teach, and encourage a worship life for the home.

Although a devotional life that is centered in the home is well documented in the New Testament, it seems to have lost its valued place in the church in America. One reason for this decline may be a negative reaction to a harsh and authoritarian family devotional life experienced by some in the older generations. Whatever the reason, few in today's congregations have a clear understanding of or models for a devotional life in the home.

Tadpole Tale: Say grace, Jeremy

David once asked his 13-year-old son, Jeremy, to say grace before dinner. Usually, he would simply say, "Grace," and wait for a reaction. This time, however, he immediately began a prayer. Dad was initially impressed, thinking that some progress was being made in his son's faith life until he heard Jeremy's prayer, "Lord, we don't thank you for this food because we bought it ourselves. Amen." Dad was shocked by his prayer and gave him a most serious stare, to which Jeremy responded, "Just kidding."

Jeremy's prayer gives a light-hearted illustration of a huge concern and struggle within most Christian homes: How do Christians foster a faith life, especially a devotional life, in the home? Although congregations are providing more guidance for a devotional life in the home, the majority of individuals and larger household communities are intimidated, uninformed, and generally inexperienced at a devotional life—even in such basic practices as a table grace before dinner. People have very little training, are often biblically illiterate, and are not exactly sure what to do or say at mealtime, bedtime, or any other time when prayer, Bible reading, and worship in the home would be fitting.

It is ironic that we stumble in doing devotions, for nearly every survey of the American people points to a deep yearning and spiritual curiosity within us. The Search Institute reports that 92 percent of Americans "are certain that God exists."[1] Yet, Americans seem to be uncertain as to how to connect with God and "one-third of adults believe that through 'meditation and self-discipline I come to know that all spiritual truth and wisdom is within me.'"[2] The question is: How can we fill this yearning with Christian devotional practices?

 ### Lily Pad Roots: Staying in touch

A devotional life is a way to "practice the presence of God" (language used by Brother Lawrence, a seventeenth-century French monk) through the word of God. As such, the devotional life is more an awareness and way of life than a formula for accomplishing a certain task. Using the Word of God means more than reading the Bible, although it certainly includes this. The word of God is first Jesus Christ, the living Word that became flesh and lived among people (John 1:14). The word of God is also the message of God that reveals God's will and work through Jesus Christ (1 Thessalonians 2:13; see also 1:2-8). Therefore, a devotional life is essentially a way of living in the world connected to the saving work and message of Jesus Christ; the intersection between the eternal with the mundane in a way that personalizes God's saving work and word. But one's devotional life is always connected to the larger body of Christ. This understanding of a devotional life includes, but is not limited to, public worship, bedtime prayers, Bible reading and study, table grace, evening and morning prayers, and praying alone at any time of the day or night. All of these occasions are opportunities for the Word of God to be "at work in you believers" (1 Thessalonians 2:13).

Tadpole Tale: How does one engage in a devotional life?

Most households need help *staying in touch through* acts of prayer and the language of faith in daily life. One congregation, which has 200 weddings per year, offers monthly pre-marriage workshops as part of its ministry. Each month a new group of couples come together to reflect upon and discuss issues pertinent to a healthy and satisfying marriage. They learn about and practice sound communication and conflict resolution skills. Family-of-origin issues are explored; intimacy and sexuality are discussed. As the workshop moves forward, a climate of trust and warmth develops.

People become engaged in meaningful conversations with their partners as well as others attending the workshop. But when it comes time to discuss the deepest intimacy of all, the spiritual life, the couples are mute. Eventually they acknowledge that it is difficult to talk about their understanding of God or how to live their lives in a way that reflects their religious convictions. They had not experienced this side of family life in their own families of origin and had no examples. It was not that they were opposed to the topic or disinterested. They were simply inexperienced in the spiritual life of the home. They ask for examples and want information, but it is a world they have seldom explored. We live in a time and a place that is largely unfamiliar with a healthy spirituality grounded in a Christian devotional life. Family devotions connect the generations with faith, hope, and love in a world that speaks and operates from a different basis than the gospel of Jesus Christ.

Lily Pad Roots: A battle is raging

The tension between the unique message of the gospel and the many other messages promoted in the culture makes personal, family, and even corporate devotions an important task and challenge. Indeed, one must ask if a devotional life of some sort is really an option in this culture. In a consumer-based society, the advertising industry wants to direct our devotion to things rather than God. The challenge for the congregation and the home is to teach and promote a Christian devotional life as a vehicle to the real source of life's fulfillment, Jesus Christ.

Ephesians 6:10-17 describes the formidable task of a life devoted to the Christian faith. The image used in this text pictures a battle "against the authorities . . . against the spiritual forces of evil in the heavenly places" (Ephesians 6:12). In a world that marches to its own drummer, neutrality is not an option. One cannot escape the fact that the church is counter-cultural. The church preaches, teaches, and believes in a source of truth, hope, and life that is not in synch with the larger society. Just as the church is counter-cultural, so is a Christian devotional life counter-cultural. Through such faith practices, the word of God is at work in the Christian community and places Christians in opposition to other dominant messages of the culture such as Jeremy's feigned prayer of unthankfulness: "We don't thank you because we bought it ourselves."

Tadpole Tale: Get a Bible into their hands

Part of the counter-cultural life of the church is to read, study, and reflect upon the message of the Bible. Our lives are bombarded by messages. God's word in the Bible offers the counter-cultural message that the church seeks to sing, pray, teach, preach, imagine, and live. Again, a motivating factor for opening the Bible and learning what is inside has to do with trusted relationships.

Carolyn was a second-year seminary student in the fall of 1990 when "Desert Shield" became "Desert Storm." Her brother's National Guard unit was put on notice that they would be called up at some point in the near future. The orders came in mid-December. They would travel to a neighboring state the first week of January where they would participate in Special Forces training, and then leave the country by mid-to-late January.

Late one afternoon in mid-January, Carolyn answered her phone and was surprised to hear her brother's voice. He said he didn't have much time, but he needed to make a special request: Would Carolyn send him a Bible, a full Bible, not just a "New Testament and Psalms?" (He figured the Old Testament might become pretty important where he was going.) It needed to be small enough to fit in the front thigh pocket of his fatigues. Carolyn agreed to his request. Then her brother said, "I need it to be here in less than three days. We leave in three days." She told him that the only Bible she could get on such a short notice that fit those specifications was one that she had been using for her personal devotions and Bible study. She had underlined many verses and even scribbled a few notes in the tiny margins. He said if she could part with it, he would really appreciate it, and he would give it back when he returned. Carolyn sent it express overnight mail.

Except for a couple of phone calls home when he left, Carolyn's brother did not correspond with anyone until two weeks prior to his return on Memorial Day weekend. A few weeks after his return, Carolyn was finally able to visit with him. In the course of their conversation he said, "I'm sorry, I can't return your Bible to you . . . I gave it away." He had been reading it when a young member of his unit asked what he was reading so intently, and assumed it must be pretty important since it had been underlined and there were visible scrawls in the margins. Carolyn's brother told her that the

Bible had been the tool that had allowed him an opportunity to share his faith with this young soldier. After several conversations, the young man asked how to be baptized. They found the chaplain, had some conversations with him, and the young soldier was baptized. Carolyn's brother was the only sponsor. He said that as a sponsor he felt compelled to give a baptismal gift to the young man and that the best thing he could give was his sister's marked-up Bible. He concluded, "I'll pay you for it, and I'd like to know where to get one." Carolyn responded, "You can have the one I bought to replace the one I sent you, and you don't have to pay me a cent. You have already paid me plenty."

Five years later, in the spring of 1996, her brother's son (her godchild) graduated from high school one weekend, was married the next weekend, and was inducted into the U.S. Army the following weekend. Carolyn knew that because of distance and other responsibilities, she would be unable to attend any of those events, so a week prior to graduation, she called to talk with her nephew. She asked what he wanted from her for a graduation/wedding gift. His swift reply was, "A Bible, just like the one you gave dad." She said she would order one and have it mailed directly to him. He said, "No, I mean just like the one with all the underlining and notes and stuff—all the same verses!" Carolyn was stunned. She managed to stutter out a response. Yes, she could send a Bible like the one she had given his dad. She still had the one she had purchased after his dad's return. She had used it for personal devotions and Bible study, but she didn't know if she had underlined all the same verses or made the same notes. He said he didn't care if it was exactly the same or not, but he would like it if he could have it. He knew the one she gave his dad had meant a lot to his dad. She sent her Bible to her nephew.

Whether the Bible of a sister, an aunt, a friend, or from a grandmother's estate, the life history, thoughts, scribblings, and other notations gleaned from those pages can be precious and powerful testimonies. Family and friends sometimes give Bibles and inscribe personal thoughts inside the cover and along the margins of favorite passages. These, too, are ways to foster a devotional life of Bible reading that can influence the faith of another. In this way, people can engage in a unique form of Bible study that links people over time, stimulating wonderment, awe, and a faith bond between and among the generations.

Tadpole Tale: Time to get real; time to make disciples

It seems everywhere we teach youth and family ministry concepts and strategies, the issue of family devotions creates controversy and conversation. While leading a workshop of high school youth, adult church leaders, and parents, we suggested that a key activity for families is to practice daily devotions together. One member of the group blasted, "Get real, you guys, we don't even eat meals together!" That sentiment often lays just beneath the surface of many a conversation on the topic of family devotions. Whether the person is on a congregational staff, is a lay leader, or is an infrequent worship attendee, the concern is the same. Other priorities and cultural values are in contention with the simple discipline of sitting together in prayer.

The issue is as simple and direct as time and priorities. The God who gives us abundant life, also gives us abundant time. But how do we use that time? One parent called the confirmation director at her congregation expressing frustration that her daughter could not fit confirmation class into her active, worthwhile, and productive schedule. (The congregation offered five different times a week in which youth could participate in confirmation, but none of the times fit this active youth's life.)

The confirmation director anguished over the call, wondering if a tutorial approach could work, but concluded that in a congregation that offered five options, obviously the caller's priorities put confirmation at the bottom of the list. The director told the parent, "As parents, I know we always make choices according to our priorities. If and when confirmation becomes a priority for your family, I would warmly welcome your daughter into our program."

Jesus made it clear that his coming will not bring peace, although the church often refrains from this message. In fact, Jesus' entry into our lives may well bring a sword that could divide homes and communities (and challenge our schedules; see Matthew 10:34-39 and Luke 12:51-53). Jesus does not lower the bar of expectations for discipleship, but raises it by suggesting an all-or-nothing quality to the Christian life that simply cannot be diluted by other interests, values, or beliefs. In the Sermon on the Mount, Jesus flatly states that one cannot serve two masters (see Matthew 6:24). Following Jesus brings abundant life by making it the exclusive gift of the one who is the author of all of created life. This creating, redeeming, and sustaining God is the source of all that is beautiful, loving, wise, and eternal.

Often adults attending our workshops tell us their kids blow this stuff off, or a spouse seems totally uninterested, or they are laughed at for trying to give a spiritual center to the home. Truly, the issues are not easy, but clearly illustrate that the cutting edge of evangelism lays within our own homes and around our own dinner tables. We all struggle with schedules, priorities, family and friendship ties, as well as our own doubts about the essential value of the Christian faith. At times we all fail. Such wrestling has always been an integral part of the Christian journey.

To those who say, "Get real" or those who scoff or laugh we respond, "Whose reality are you talking about? Do you really want or intend to go through life without spiritual anchoring? Does your reality make room for the way, the truth, and the life? Do you believe—do you even want to believe—that the Christian faith makes a difference? If so, give the devotional life a chance! Raise the bar and do not lower it. See what a differ-ence such a commitment can make. Give it a chance to shape your sense of delight and hope in a world that continually sends the message, 'You are not good enough . . . yet.'"

Devotional practices have a way of revealing what is true and what is false and where our priorities really lie. Thus, the Christian life needs to be constantly created and recre-ated—and defended—by the work of the Holy Spirit living in our devotional practices. It is the stuff that makes disciples for Jesus.

Lily Pad Roots: Attitudes, goals, and behaviors

Colossians 3:15-17 describes the life devoted to God in terms of attitudes, goals, and behaviors. The attitudes are those of thanksgiving (3:15) and gratitude (3:16). Contrast these attitudes with the words of Jeremy's prayer ("Lord, we don't thank you for this food because we bought it ourselves. Amen"). Which attitude is more predomi-nant in our culture? Which attitude do we want our children to have? Which attitude do you most often reflect?

The goal is to "let the peace of Christ rule in your hearts" (Colossians 3:15) in such a way that in "whatever you do, in word or deed," you will "do everything in the name of the Lord Jesus, giving thanks to God the Father through him" (3:17). Contrast this goal of peace with the goals we reflect. Due to the competitive nature of our culture and eco-nomic system, for example, many Christians feel torn between this goal and the expec-tations they must live by in other cultural and work settings. (This is even true of those who work in the public church. No one seems to escape the malady.) Without exercising good devotional practices, it is quite likely that the goal of Christ's peace will fade into the background because of the volume (both quantity and decibels) of messages that push us in other directions with anger, self-doubt, and anguish.

The behavior that lends itself to this attitude and goal includes teaching and admonishing one another as well as singing "psalms, hymns, and spiritual songs to God" (Colossians 3:16). All of this is to be understood within the context of prayer, as Colossians later states, "Devote yourselves to prayer, keeping alert in it with thanksgiving" (4:2; see also Philippians 4:4-8). Note how attitudes and goals relate to behavior. What a relief to live a consistent lifestyle where public and private practices are the same, in contrast to the compartmentalization so common in American culture in which public attitudes and behaviors are different than private practices. A healthy devotional life helps one be consistent, and that alone can bring peace.

The exciting—and challenging—part of all of this is that no single way to properly develop a meaningful devotional life for the home exists. Whatever shape it takes, it needs to be connected to the congregation (public worship), and the practices that are consistent with the faith tradition represented by the congregation. For example, one simple suggestion is to have in the home multiple copies of the worship book(s) and hymnal(s) used by the congregation. Hymns are sung prayers, and hymnal and worship books also often include specific prayers, Bible readings, and prayer liturgies that are intended for the home or can be adapted for individual or family use. *Lutheran Book of Worship,* for example, provides recommended adaptations of morning and evening prayer for use in the home or in other small-group settings. Although most active congregational members are not familiar with these resources as devotional tools, numerous devotional ideas can emerge from congregational worship books and hymnals. An added benefit to congregations is that these worship forms assist parishioners to build devotional lives in their own homes. Worshipers well versed in their congregation's worship strengthen not only the devotional life of the home, but also the public worship life of the congregation.

The critical issue is that the public, congregational church is an active teacher and supporter of the worship life of the home. Congregations that help homes explore ways to pray, times to pray, and even places to pray in the home, go a long way to help family life be rich soil for passing on the faith. One easy way for congregations to address this topic is to make the promotion of home devotions a fundamental goal of a congregation's Christian education, especially adult Christian education.

Tadpole Tale: Using topical books for devotions

New and unanticipated ways of family worship can emerge in our homes. In the summer of 2000 one of our families had the opportunity to meet the great church leader and activist, Bishop Desmond Tutu. We visited briefly with him, got a photograph, and had him sign his book. As a result of this encounter, we read from his book each night after supper as our evening devotions. He challenges us to think of the global world, issues of racism, and the power of reconciliation.

Tadpole Tale: Silence, meditation, and reflection work

Youth can warm up to the idea of the spiritual life. In the mid-1980s, Paul tried an experiment at the Bible camp he was directing. Lutheran camp directors had been using the *Taizé form of worship and meditation*, a very contemplative form of worship that uses icons, incense, long periods of silence, Scripture reading, and repetitive songs as tools for focusing on Christ. He and his staff decided that they would introduce this form of worship to junior-high youth at camp—a high-risk idea. Would they cooperate? Would they laugh? Would there be lots of body sounds during the silence? To the amazement of the camp staff, the kids loved it. They would sit in this contemplative worship for up to 45 minutes!

David had a similar experience on retreat with one of his eighth-grade confirmation classes. The first evening he led them through a guided imagery based on Matthew 6:33, "But strive first for the kingdom of God and his righteousness, and all these things will be given to you as well." The next day the students asked him to end the retreat with another guided imagery. David, almost in protest, noted that such relaxation and meditation might put them to sleep at a late hour. The students quickly acknowledged the likelihood of this and welcomed it. They thought, "What a way to end the day."

Recent studies by Mark Yaconelli at San Francisco Theological Seminary demonstrate the importance of contemplative devotions as an important way of engaging in youth ministry. Given the proper instruction and a safe environment, young people are willing to explore spiritual practices that impact their lives.

Young adults also appreciate a deeper devotional life. So-called GenX congregations such as Mars Hill Church in Seattle place a strong emphasis on contemplation, intense Scripture study, and reflective music. After visiting this church on a Sunday evening, one of the nearly 300 young adults present was asked if all the services were so *somber*. She looked at the questioner with a flicker of anger and said, "This isn't somber; this is our spirituality." While some may perceive the contemplative service as somber, a whole community of young adults experience deep communion with Christ.

Lily Pad Roots: Follow-up care and attentiveness

The opportunity for people to experience different types of home devotions before determining what works best is important. Follow-up is critical. Old patterns of neglect die hard, and new disciplines take time to become part of one's personal or family routine. People need the ongoing support and attention that indicate that their lives, relationships, and faith are important. Checking in with individuals and households to see how things are going is one way to communicate care and support.

Consistency and attentiveness to what's working and what's not working in people's lives is essential to training in Christian discipleship. A by-product of Jesus' presence with his followers was this kind of attentiveness to faith formation. Contemporary examples of this careful attention to change in people's lives are small group ministries and recovery groups, which offer support and accountability as people seek to change and mature in their daily lives and habits.

Households also need resources. Besides specific devotional magazines and books, a rich variety of resources exist to help support and encourage a devotional life. Resources promoted for the home become the curriculum for the home just as other resources are developed and promoted for the faith formation in the congregation.[3] Music tapes and compact discs, storybook Bibles, children's faith story books, inspirational and educational books, and games that reinforce the life of faith are all resources that can help families and congregations enrich the faith-lives of children, youth, and adults.

Parents and grandparents are especially interested in knowing what resources work for children at different ages and how such tools might be used. Not only is it valuable for congregations to identify resources and make them available to adults, it is also important to help these adults learn how to use them as part of their cross-generational faith life. Adults who have taken the responsibility to be a godparent (baptismal sponsor) or faith mentor are increasingly looking for faith-forming resources (sometimes given to their charges as gifts) that they can use with children and youth on their mutual faith journey.

Training people for a meaningful faith-life in the home is a critical ministry that congregations can provide for children, youth, and adults. As an example, some parents need to be shown how to read to their children since it may be an experience that they do not remember having themselves. *Reading to children is critical.* Early childhood development specialists point out that a child who spends 1,000 hours in the lap of an adult who is reading to them will do much better in school when they enter kindergarten. They bond, they learn, they appreciate books, and they could be learning Bible stories at the same time. A combination of accessible resources and suggestions regarding the devotional life of the home is a strategic move for congregations and an important means to develop an effective partnership with the home to pass on the faith between generations.

Lily Pad Roots: Adult insecurities

An obvious challenge to the establishment and development of a devotional life in the home is dealing with the insecurities and biblical illiteracy of adults. A fundamental goal, therefore, is to move people beyond the sense of threat or intimidation in their own faith journeys. One way to do this is to recognize that parents and grandparents can learn with children. For example, a storybook Bible read to a three-year-old can also become an adult textbook. Reading from a storybook Bible to a child sitting on the lap of an adult is a non-threatening yet educational opportunity to learn the biblical stories that form the foundation of the Christian tradition, language, and faith for the adult.

Reading to, and being in conversation with, a child can help an adult begin or continue the journey of life-long Christian education. Learning the content of the Bible and raising questions are all part of the journey of faith. Martin Luther himself can act as an example for insecure adults. He confessed that he did not understand the first line of the Lord's Prayer or the Apostles' Creed, but did not give up. He stated in the Large Catechism that he needed to study his faith and pray with his own little children, Hans and Lena. If this remarkable figure in Christian history struggled with the basics and learned with and from children, maybe today's adults can be freed to do the same.

One of the fundamental challenges for individuals, households, and larger family and friendship ties is beginning the journey. It takes a great deal of courage and humility to walk down a path that has not been walked before, so it helps to practice devotional methods with others as part of the public, congregational ministry. Congregational leaders make too many assumptions about people's ability to hear an idea and then practice it at home. People need to see the practice and practice it in an environment where instruction and coaching can make the devotional life more doable, meaningful, and enjoyable. A baseball coach doesn't tell a child to go home and practice the sport. Rather, the coach shows the child how to swing a bat, how to throw the ball, and how to catch a fly ball or field a grounder. Maybe we should see our pastors and other congregational leaders in a similar fashion: as spiritual coaches, not just spiritual cheerleaders.

The congregation can diminish some of the burden of initiating a devotional life in the home simply by recommending that households pursue this aspect of their Christian faith. Complex family histories and emotional roadblocks often need to be overcome before many families can engage in family devotions, especially when families include adolescents and young adults. A variety of cross-generational dynamics can inhibit parent or child from trying to explore some form of a devotional life. A teen who has not experienced prior parental interest in family faith nurture may sense awkwardness and a feeling of hypocrisy. As teenagers explore their own sense of independence, cross-generational power struggles can ensue. Parents, too, may feel awkward or simply embarrassed or guilty about not knowing how to guide devotional life in the home.

One pastor addressed these inhibitions overtly by telling parents to "blame" him for having to fulfill in-home devotional assignments given to the youth. He said playfully to the parents, "Tell them I'm mean, or not very caring or interested in the ideas and feelings of the children and youth in the home. Tell them whatever you want or need to, but put the burden on me and just do it." The pastor understood his role in addressing the anguish experienced by many parents and youth. He recognized the sensitivities that are strained in the home around the very intimate territory of family spirituality. This was his attempt to level the emotional playing field and make it just a little bit easier for families to try something new, something powerful, something very intimate, yet something unnerving for many people.

Because a devotional life can seem both intimidating and overwhelming, it is best to help people begin (or continue) this quest with simple steps. One place to begin is to recommend the use of a table grace. If need be, people can select a time and place to begin this devotional practice. Perhaps it is once a week at the Sunday dinner table. Whatever it is, many people need help to find a place and a time to begin.

Jeremy's playful prayer ("Dear Lord, we don't thank you for this food because we bought it ourselves. Amen") is valuable in that it clearly represents the attitude of an unbelieving world. It is the prayer that is not prayed with words, but with silence, the silence of not offering a table grace at all. When people receive into their bodies the stuff of creation that keeps them alive, and do not give thanks to the God of creation, the prayer they are implicitly offering is, "Lord, we don't thank you for this food because we bought it ourselves." A table grace may not be the whole of a devotional life, but it can be an important first word. (Even many active members of congregations need help to begin using table graces at home.) Whatever guidance, instruction, and strategies are offered within a congregation to assist the devotional life of the home, it is necessary in our post-Christian culture to locate meaningful ways to practice the presence of God with the Word of God.

Tadpole Tale: Starting out right

Life cycle moments like weddings, funerals, and births provide opportunities to discover or rediscover the power of a devotional life for the home; daily routines do so as well. One pastor decided to apply the Four Key practices to a wedding service. Like many of her colleagues, she realized that newlyweds were often ill equipped to begin or sustain the spiritual life in the home. Convinced that spiritual intimacy is the deepest intimacy of all, she began the prayer section of the service with a statement to the couple and all gathered saying that while the wedding prayers were an important part of the service, prayers for marriages and families were even more important in the home. She asked the couple to commit themselves to begin that very night with prayers for their marriage.

Then, to start them off, she gave the couple an envelope with prayers and scripture she had personally written for their first two days of marriage. So emphatic was she about this point that she also gave copies to the best man and the matron of honor in case the wedding couple lost theirs during the day's activities. She suggested that the best man and matron of honor, as part of their responsibilities, could pray the prayers as well for the next two nights. The scriptures and prayers written for the wedding couple were described as models that could help them begin their deepest journey of intimacy, their spiritual journey.

The pastor tried this idea because she was resolute that couples have resources and models for nurturing their faith journey, and that they begin the journey on the first night of their marriage. What amazed the pastor was the reaction of those gathered. The bride was so touched by the personal gift of prayers that she cried. The father of the bride later told the pastor that he was doing fine throughout the entire wedding service until that moment. He wept. As soon as the pastor walked out of the building following the service a couple approached her saying they had never seen that done before. They were moved by the powerful gesture and wanted to know if they could get a copy of the scriptures and prayers to pray that night and the next along with the wedding couple. At the wedding reception many people approached her to comment on the meaningfulness of those prayers.

People are interested in a meaningful life of faith, but they often do not know how to begin. This simple addition to the wedding service made a powerful point that was supported and praised by many people. The strong and very positive reaction received by the pastor made her wonder more about the possibilities and impact of the prayers. She has decided to continue that practice in the future, except now she wants to offer scriptures and prayers for each night of the honeymoon. She is considering inviting family and friends of the couple to write their own prayers and add them to hers. She wants to make the entire devotional packet available to all who would like to use the scriptures and prayers during the days that follow the wedding service as a way to continue their faithful and loving support of the newlywed couple.

Tadpole Tale: Table grace evangelism

We began and will end this chapter by talking about table graces. Jeremy's prayer at the beginning of the chapter is the prayer of a secular culture. We need to pray the prayers of gratitude when we eat. It is the means by which we stay alive.

One family's story gives a good example of how meaningful table grace can be and how it serves the evangelistic nature of the church. One family begins each meal with the tradition of a simple prayer, "Thank you God for the food we eat! Amen." This prayer, sung to the tune of *Ode to Joy,* is one the children invented when they were very small (this is a good example of how treasured family traditions often get established). At the end of the meal, the family prays a prayer from the mother's family tradition, "Oh give thanks unto God for God is good and God's mercy endures forever," followed by the Lord's Prayer.

Often, friends of the children join the family for meals. Once, the 16-year-old son brought a girlfriend home who was not active in any church and whose family rarely ate together. She joined the family in the meal preparation and then sat quietly while the family said the table grace. At the end of the meal the family concluded in prayer, as usual. The son later told his mother that he had a conversation with his girlfriend about spirituality, triggered by the table grace. The girl commented, "When I get older I think I'll be more spiritual. That's not a part of our family and I feel I'm missing something." The mother asked her son how he responded. He laughed and said, "I told her my family is too religious and that when I'm older I'm going to be less spiritual." They both laughed. Although the relationship between the two teens ended before more spiritual conversation could take place, this experience points out that a devotional life is deeply evangelical as well. It's a great way of witnessing.

Croaks, Ribbits, and Hops

A primary task of congregations is to help households experience a daily life strengthened by the word of God. Many models and resources can be suggested to help individuals and families in this important ministry. Besides those already suggested, the following are a few more ideas.

Bedtime and mealtime are the two critical times to do devotions. A Bible camp director encouraged the counselors to make sure they do a closing devotion at the end of the day. Often these devotions were done with the lights out and only a candle burning (Bible camps often call this moment the "sacred candle"). Evaluations from campers demonstrated that this was one of the most popular things done at camp. So much for those who say, "Get real!"

A choir director from a congregation spoke of the devotional ritual his family practices at bedtime. They pray the "please, sorry, and thank you" method. The prayer begins with the parent and child identifying what they want to ask of God (please), comparable to the *Kyrie* in the historic liturgy of the church. Then they pray about the things they regret (sorry). This is called the Confession in the liturgy. Finally, they pray for that for which they are thankful (thank you). In the liturgy this is called the Gloria. By going through this sequence each night, the parent learns a lot about the child's day, and the family makes a connection to the greater church through the structure of the prayer.

Again, the *FaithTalk* cards mentioned earlier in this book are ideal for use in the car as faith discussion starters. It is also a regular practice in our homes to do a few cards whenever we have company. We have spent hours with friends, students, and colleagues in hilarious, playful, and non-threatening conversation simply by responding to the questions on the cards.

Another great resource for mental imaging is the series *Imaging the Word*.[4] This three-volume set follows the church lectionary (the selection of Bible texts read each Sunday) and provides poems, art, and photographs to help give insight into the lectionary themes.

A personal and family devotional life can take place at any place, at any time, and in any way that works. The point is that devotional time works best as a practice, a discipline that one consciously enters.

- Congregations can help by teaching and encouraging different ways to enter into a devotional life. How can your congregation (or Christian study group) help you develop and maintain a devotional life that makes a difference in your daily life?
- Wedding and baby showers, or weddings, births, and funerals are all occasions that would be appropriate to offer a gift that nurtures the faith of individuals and households.[5]

Finally, we offer the following simple outline as a possible way to organize your day devotionally.

- When you awake say the following as you inhale: "The Lord is my Shepherd." When you exhale say, "I shall not want." Do this for a few minutes as you lie in bed.
- When you wash in the bathroom look in the mirror as you splash water on your face and say, "I am God's child through my baptism." Make the sign of the cross on your forehead and do the same for other family members.
- At your breakfast time say prayers and take a minute for a brief reading of a psalm or other scripture.
- As you or family members leave for the day, stop at the door and pray for God's guidance and light to shine through you. Make sure to give a special ritual departure.
- At lunch offer a mealtime grace before you eat.
- At supper offer a table grace before eating and consider using a brief word of praise following the meal. After the meal use a devotional resource such as the Bible, a devotional book, or *FaithTalk* cards.
- At the end of the day pray with each family member as they lie down to rest. You can do this activity if you live alone as well. The "please, sorry, thank you" prayer model works wonderfully across the generations. This recommendation is intended for single people, too. Remember, family relationships can include friends, neighbors, and others who are part of your faith journey, people who are not necessarily connected to you by birth, marriage, or adoption.
- When an individual finishes school (from elementary school to college and graduate school) or begins a new school or work setting, participate in a blessing/sending service that enriches the moment with the encouragement of God's presence and promises as well as your own words and gestures of care and support.

- Prayer while on a walk in the neighborhood or out in nature is invigorating for the body, mind, and soul.
- Use special occasions like holidays, beginning or ending a vacation, sending a loved one off to a new venture, and life cycle transitions as opportunities to explore the powerful bond you have with others through prayer, Scripture, conversation, and rituals and traditions.
- Explore or rediscover family worship moments for the seasons of the church year. Use an advent calendar and candles. Sing hymns and read the nativity story in Matthew or Luke as you gather around the Christmas tree (and bless the Christmas tree while you are at it). Do a house blessing for Epiphany. Recommit yourself to the Lenten disciplines of prayer, fasting, and almsgiving. Celebrate Easter with an Easter egg hunt that includes prayers and Scripture readings. Do intentional acts of love and service to others, including strangers. Greet family and friends with the Easter greeting: "Christ is risen! Christ is risen, indeed! Alleluia!"
- Explore a devotional life with a trusted friend or family member. People on a common journey can do a lot to free one another to try what might be more difficult to attempt alone.

NOTES

1. Gene Roehlkepartain, *The Teaching Church* (Nashville, Abingdon, 1993), 44.
2. Ibid., 45.
3. *FaithLife in the Home,* developed by The Youth & Family Institute (www.youthandfamilyinstitute.org), compiles devotional resources gathered from nearly 50 different publishing houses. The selected resources have been reviewed and chosen on the basis of their ability to nurture the faith life of the home at any point in the life cycle. Congregations can make the items from the *FaithLife in the Home* available directly to the home by establishing the "Resource and Gift Center" as a ministry of the congregation for the home.
4. *Imaging the Word: An Arts and Lectionary Resource,* vol 1-3, Kenneth T. Lawrence, Jann Cather Weaver, Roger Wedell, Susan A. Blain, Sharon Iverson Gouwens, Catherine O'Callaghan, and Grand Spradling, eds. (Cleveland: United Church Press).
5. See *FaithLife in the Home* for numerous examples.

CHAPTER ELEVEN

Frogs for the Pond,
Key 3—Service

Frogs need ponds, and ponds need frogs. Frogs without ponds are lifeless and ponds without frogs lack the sounds, water ripples, and multiple life forms that frogs bring. Frogs and ponds are made for each other and neither is completely healthy without the other.

The church frog exists to support life and encourage the health of the whole pond, our God-given world. The healthy church frog has strong, energized, and motivated legs, a unifying, passionate heart beating in the torso, and a thinking, wise, and insightful head to live in the world and exist for the world. Paul addresses this issue in 1 Corinthians, where he chastised the Corinthian Christians for immorality that exceeded that of the local culture. (Ancient Corinth was a port city known for its raunchy, scandalous, and outrageous activity.) The Corinthian Christians understood one half of the gospel— that their sins were forgiven and they lived by God's grace through Jesus Christ. Unfortunately, they had not made the connection between the gospel and the need for themselves to behave in such a way as to give honor and praise to God and uplift the community. The Corinthian position was "because God loves and forgives me I can do anything I want."

To the Corinthians, Paul wrote, "All things are lawful . . . but not all things are benefi-cial . . ." (1 Corinthians 6:12). Paul wanted to affirm the essential nature of the gospel (we are forgiven daily!), but to also point to the fruit of living in this gospel—to build up the community and to serve and support others. One who claims the gospel of forgiveness without doing acts of service is like a frog trying to live without the pond. The faith is dead and soon so will be the frog. At the same time, one who does acts of service in order to receive or earn the gospel of forgiveness is like a frog who thinks it is his responsibility to fill the pond with water. The frog has forgotten that the rain and water are gifts from God that collect in the pond and for which the frog can only be grateful. The gospel is God's ongoing, undeserved outpouring of love and forgiveness to which we can only respond in gratitude through lives of service to others.

Service is the third key to a lifestyle that creates healthy church homes, congregations, neighborhoods, communities, and bears witness to Jesus Christ in the world.

Tadpole Tale: Service changes lives

When parent and child together perform service activities, the child sees the parent's capability, faith, and values in action. The cross-generational bond takes place not only in the service event, but in the retelling of the event through the years. We call this the "ah-ha, remember when!" syndrome. All families experience this syndrome. These stories are the family's collective memories of adventures, struggles, experiences, and times together; the lore that holds a family together. By doing service together lore is created. When told over and over again, this lore affirms family faith, values, and identity for all family members, which is a critical dynamic in the shaping power of service. In other words, the narration serves as proclamation. It is a *sermon* that enlarges one's sense of connectedness to a greater good and a heightened sense of belonging.

Truly one of the most difficult and sad moments in Paul's ministry took place in Denver, Colorado. A couple in the congregation he was serving had given birth to a marvelous little girl. She was all the more special because it took them nine years to conceive. She was to her parents the gift for which they had longed, and she was the center of their universe.

One evening, this couple brought their new daughter to a party thrown by one of the congregational members. It was the first "show off" night for them and all "oohed" and "aahed" over this baby. The evening was festive and joyful. At one point the mother took her daughter to a bedroom to lay her down. Fifteen minutes later she went to check her. She came rushing down from the bedroom with her limp baby girl in her arms. Her daughter was pale and without movement.

Paul and his wife Elaine began emergency CPR on the child while her mother looked on in horror. Those were anguishing moments that seemed to last an eternity. The efforts to revive the child failed; she died of Sudden Infant Death Syndrome. All who were together in the home were devastated. Paul vividly recalls sitting with these parents crying, praying, reading scripture, and holding them while Elaine gently rubbed the mother's back for well over an hour. Months after the funeral, Paul and Elaine met with this same couple. The mother, remembering that evening, commented that she felt most supported by Elaine's back rub. That gentle touch of assurance and quiet presence was a significant ministry to her.

Many years later Elaine and Paul were at their daughter's elementary school listening to student poetry. One of the girls read a poem she had written for a friend who had recently been killed in a car accident. The poem expressed her loss and sadness, and almost everyone on stage and in the audience wept with her. During the reading of this poem, Paul saw something he had not witnessed since the death of the baby girl. Amber, his daughter, who was sitting next to the poet as she read her sorrowful poem, began gently to rub her classmate's back. No one told her to do it. She instinctively reacted to her grieving friend with this caring touch. "How does she know to do that?" Paul asked himself. She's never been in this situation before, and yet she knew that a back rub is a powerful ministry for those in grief. Then Paul remembered Elaine's similar gesture so many years ago. Amber had learned from her mother. But how? Amber wasn't even born when that event took place? The lifestyle of caring service that Elaine exhibited every day in her child rearing had become a part of Amber. She learned to serve effectively by experiencing and watching her mother rub backs when human pain and sadness seemed to overwhelm. Ironically, Amber's poem shared that day was a call for her "growth spurt" to appear. She was tired of being short. Little did she know that she already stood tall in other ways.

This is the power of cross-generational service in faith formation. Studies clearly show that children and youth learn the faith by watching the adults they respect live the faith. Most significantly, service is not merely a once-a-month outing to pick up trash on the highway, or an occasional visit to a shut-in. Service is the day-in and day-out lifestyle we lead that manifests the faith in us and involves our children in the faith. Parents and families can engage in this key every day.

Lily Pad Roots: Service is a calling

Service on behalf of one's neighbor (whether friend or stranger) is the calling all are given through the life and message of Jesus Christ. The love extended by God through Christ motivates the Christian to the care and service of others. Loving deeds that respond to the needs of others represents the basis for Christian discipleship, evangelism, and stewardship. The human dimension of care and service for others and the larger created order is the human response to the providential care of God, a concrete expression of one's faith and values, and represents God's loving, gracious activity in the world.

From the beginning of the Gospel narratives, the Christian faith and life were described in terms of loving acts of service. In the Gospel of Luke, Jesus described his ministry in the language of the prophet Isaiah, and referred to a divine responsiveness to the poor, the captive, the blind, and the oppressed. This inaugural sermon by Jesus is a defining moment that offers a powerful revelation regarding the work and message of Jesus. Jesus articulated quite clearly that he came empowered by God for the needy; he came to serve. This motivation to serve stresses God's central activity of justice and mercy in the world, and embodies an essential way of life for God's people (see Micah 6:8). The Sermon on the Mount in Matthew extols a way of life filled with humility, support of others, and an awareness of God's presence in the midst of all relationships. In the sermon, Jesus expects disciples to "walk the talk." Toward the end of the Gospel, Jesus described the great judgment of the end times in terms of separating those who served the needs of others and those who did not (Matthew 25:31-46). The Gospel of John dramatically emphasizes the essential nature of loving acts of service. When Jesus washed his disciples' feet on the night in which he was betrayed by one of his own disciples (John 13), he set the standard for discipleship: service, even—or, perhaps, especially—in humbling circumstances.

The New Testament letters also reflect this essential commitment to humble service as a way of life. The gifts given by the Holy Spirit for the Christian disciple are given to serve others, especially those in the household of faith (see Romans 12:3-13; 1 Corinthians 12:4-11; Galatians 6:7-10). The letter of James is never hesitant to link good deeds with genuine faith: "Religion that is pure and undefiled before God, the Father, is this: to care for orphans and widows in their distress, and to keep oneself unstained by the world" (James 1:27). This theme is punctuated by the stark words, "So faith by itself, if it has no works, is dead" (James 2:17).

The life of service does not emerge in a vacuum but is initiated, formed, and equipped through the work of God in community. As the Tadpole Tale illustrates, the intimate space of family relationships becomes the first internship experience for disciples of Christ. It is no wonder that the New Testament uses the language of family, household, brothers and sisters, and parents and children as a basic metaphor for the Christian community. Living with and caring for others on a regular basis is very messy business, which is the crucible and testing grounds to "walk in newness of life" (Romans 6:4), to experience "our way of life" (Ephesians 2:10), and to "walk in the light" (1 John 1:7). Family life provides one of the foundational settings for the development of a life of service. Familial relationships provide a primary context in which Christians are

> to lead a life worthy of the calling to which you have been called, with all humility and gentleness, with patience, bearing with one another in love, making every effort to maintain the unity of the Spirit in the bond of peace (Ephesians 4:1-3).

Service to the world that flows out of the home has been shown to be a vital way to pass on faith from generation to generation. Children and youth are greatly influenced by what they see in the lives of others, especially parents and other family members. For a household of two or three generations to reach out to a neighbor in need (or to the unnamed faces of multitudes of hungry, homeless, or others requiring social or material assistance) leaves a lasting impression on the children and youth of the servant family. Older generations, likewise, benefit from the awareness of the value and the satisfaction of using their talents and resources to make a positive difference in the lives of others. A collection of family service memories goes a long way to promote and affirm the Christian life. It embodies the Christian ethic of "faith working through love" (Galatians 5:6).

Tadpole Tale: Hungry people

One family occasionally served a meal at the local rescue mission. They nearly always showed up to help on Christmas or New Year's Day. The parents not only understood their work as helping others, but also as a way for their two kids (Daniel, age 12, and Rozenia, age 9) to see the whole of life. The family of four would cook all the food at home and bring it to the mission where they would join others to serve 50-75 poor and homeless people. The very first time they helped at the mission, a man walked in looking rough and unkempt. He sat down at the table and Rozenia walked over to him and asked, "Which would you like, mashed potatoes or stuffing?" The man did not look at her, but simply mumbled, "Food!" The little girl was taken aback, but nevertheless, went to the counter and got the man some food. She then left the group for a time, but others were too busy to notice.

Two years later Rozenia wrote a paper for a junior high class in which she was to tell of an experience that changed her life. She wrote of this man at the rescue mission. For the first time in her life she learned of the reality of desperate hunger and poverty. After she had served this one individual, she had gone to the restroom to cry. She learned that people live in the world that cannot pick between M&M's and Skittles. Food, any food, was sufficient. She also learned that she could have an impact on that reality and serve in Jesus' name.

After reading her paper, the rest of the family came to understand the power of service in shaping her. At least for awhile, designer clothes and pop fads did not seem as important to her.

Lily Pad Roots: The importance of cross-generational service and storytelling

Merton Strommen, founder of the Search Institute, reviewed the data from the Search Institute that eventually was reported in the study *Effective Christian Education*. He observed that adults who were assessed to have a more mature faith (those who had a clearer sense of a gracious God in their lives and the desire to serve the needs of others) tended to be those who could remember doing acts of service with their parents when they were children.[1] The data suggests that family service projects have a life-long impact on children.

Tadpole Tales: From Egypt to Minnesota

One example of this comes from Al Quie, a former governor and United States senator from Minnesota. He once shared a story about growing up in Minnesota during the Great Depression, noting that it was the tradition (another of the Four Keys) of his rural community to welcome homeless people (called hobos during this period) at the back door of the farmhouse and give them a hot meal. He acknowledged that his own dad did not do that. Instead, when homeless people came on their property, his dad would welcome them into the house, seat them at their dining room table and eat with them. Quie's father showed a sense of respect and care for the individuals that went beyond addressing the physical need for food. He also addressed the need to be esteemed and valued in the presence of others. It was all part of the Quie family life and faith.

This story is a memory in the life of the father's son that impacted the son's own faith development. He tells the story with warmth. It means something to the boy who would grow up to live out his Christian servanthood as a governor, U.S. senator, and leader in prison ministry and youth ministry across the country.

It is not simply an act of service that shapes a person's life, but also the memory of the event that functions as an interpretation of what is important, meaningful, and worth believing. God's grace and mercy was present and active in the life of a father. The power and impact of that display of God's grace went far beyond that moment in time in the 1930s. When God acts, it is meant to be remembered, retold, and to shape the lives of future generations. When God introduced the 10 plagues in Egypt to free God's enslaved people it was a moment in time not to be forgotten, but to be a precious memory to an entire people for future generations. As God told Moses, these divine acts in history occur so that "you may tell your children and grandchildren how I have made fools of the Egyptians and what signs I have done among them—so that you may know that I am the LORD" (Exodus 10:2). The memory of God's activity in history, whether in Egypt or on a Minnesota farm, lives on as a story retold for others to hear to shape their faith and values, and form their character.

The broader American culture, as well as the church, has learned to value service learning activities. So much in life can be learned outside of classrooms and books. Life-shaping moments are likely to occur while assisting others in a nursing home or serving at a soup kitchen or any number of other activities that get into the face and consciousness of developing lives. The challenge, however, is that service activities can fade in the memory of those who serve, or it can be redefined as "kid's stuff," something that will be outgrown in adulthood so that the "real" activity of earning money can be pursued.

Tadpole Tales: Telling stories matters!

Young people who participate in mission trips to inner cities, rural communities, or foreign countries often report that these are life-shaping moments. What is often discovered is that the recipients of care are the ones who really know what is essential to life and how to share it. These persons usually powerfully influence those who come to serve. But teachable moments such as these can be lost if the events are not experienced with older generations, including parents, to confirm that this is a way of life for all of life. Further, these teachable moments can be lost if the stories are not told again and again as part of the cross-generational experience and become part of one's conscious and formative faith history.

Each year, a youth pastor in the state of Washington took his youth group to Mexico during spring break to construct facilities at a nursing home. The young people were always moved by the needs, love, and warmth of the people, and by their own ability to make a difference in the lives of others. According to the pastor, the trip is always an emotional and spiritual high for these youth. On a typical return trip to Washington, the bus would always be abuzz with excited storytelling and reviews of the awesome week, but the pastor also noted that the excited chatter dramatically shifted once the bus was within a few miles of their church. Once off the bus, he would hear many parents and other family and friends ask about the experience. To the pastor's amazement, the standard response was a simple "Fine" or "It was okay." Something was lost. The stories that had emerged on the ride home were not retold. The faith-shaping events of the week would be lost to the generations not present in Mexico. Indeed, it is likely that the memories would fade from the faith history of the youth themselves.

While it would be worthwhile to have adults join the youth in the service project in Mexico to make it a cross-generational experience, it is unrealistic to expect every parent, guardian, or mentor to be a part of the trip to Mexico, but it *is* realistic to build into the event multiple ways for the stories to be passed onto those awaiting the return of the youth. Using video, photographs, skits, worship services, and formal presentations as well as informal storytelling, families and congregation members can experience and learn what the youth did. This kind of retelling becomes a powerful means to keep the stories alive in order to shape the faith of teens and adults alike. Such storytelling is the work of the Holy Spirit to nurture faith.

Capturing and retelling stories is not new. The practice at Wilderness Canoe Base, a Christian camp in northern Minnesota, is to offer a "disclosure" time for every group that has gone on a canoe trip. Each evening the camp staff, along with the campers, gather in the chapel and those who have just returned from their trip in the Boundary Waters Canoe Area are given the opportunity to tell their stories. The humor, power, intensity, and remarkable accounts shared in community help fix these experiences permanently into the lives of the campers and staff alike. What was an experience now becomes lore, legend, and tradition.

Tadpole Tale: Service shapes families

The Orlandos became aware of the value of doing service activities together as a family through the educational and youth ministry of their congregation. As individuals, both parents and children were engaged in different acts of service in the neighborhood, their congregation, and other organizations, but nothing was done as a family. Most of the acts of service were age-segregated, and most of the serving and its impact on the family members were left unreported. The parents decided to change that. They joined with other households in their congregation periodically to work in a warehouse to package food for low-income individuals and families. The parents, children, and a larger group of cross-generational servers worked together. Some of the workers were directed by the courts to be there for community service. Others were there to gain coupons to receive food at a significant discount. Not only were the Orlandos enriched by working side-by-side with people who came from diverse backgrounds, they were also able to earn coupons for bags of groceries that they gave to others in need. The Saturdays they volunteered their time with friends, family, and strangers provided an education and a sense of community care that they had not had before.

The Orlandos were also able to use the contacts in their congregation to connect with the Nguyen family that had emigrated from Laos the year before. One of the ways they decided to help assimilate the Nguyen family to their new surroundings was to take the children trick-or-treating for Halloween. The Orlandos learned that the Nguyens had arrived arrived before Halloween the year before and that had been a frightening experience. The Nguyens had no idea why masked and screaming children were coming to their door. Once the Nguyens learned it was meant to be a playful activity and not harmful, they were willing participants, especially the children who were excited to get candy. A few days before Halloween, the weather was turning bad. The Orlandos got together with the Nguyens one more time before Halloween to make sure everything was in order. The Orlandos told the Nguyens that the children should wear gloves, coats, boots, and hats because it could snow. Mao, the mother, informed the Orlandos that her children did not have winter clothing. This information shocked the Orlando children who immediately asked, "What did your children do last winter?" Mao responded that they simply stayed inside. Within 48 hours the Orlandos had retrieved enough gloves, coats, and hats through helping agencies for the entire Nguyen family.

The stories of packaging food in the warehouse and the many family get-togethers with the Nguyens changed the Orlando family. Other lifestyles were learned. Some harsh realities about life were grasped in new and powerful ways. Ways to care and make a difference in the lives of others were taught. The value of care and new ways to be disciples of God's love in Christ became part of the fabric of the Orlando household. They found new ways to enjoy being together and being together with others. They gained a renewed sense of who the Orlandos were, how each member of the family contributed to the good of others, and how Jesus' call to serve brings healing and hope to lives. The Orlando parents came to understand that their times of service together gave them fond memories of time with their children and a richer understanding of how their Christian faith is a blessing to their home and, hopefully, to many others as well. They realized how those times together serving others have influenced their children, their choices, their values and faith, and even their careers.

When service is offered and stories are told, the motivation for serving must be made known; the serving needs to be understood as a response to the calling of Jesus and a part of Christian discipleship. *FaithFactors* research indicates that for service to be faith formative, a connection must be made between the action and the person of Jesus. One cannot assume this connection is being made. It must be stated clearly. For example, frame a service project in prayer in Jesus' name and encourage participants to articulate that they are doing this activity in response to Jesus' love (see Matthew 5:16). The vertical relationship with Jesus must be connected to the horizontal relationship with the neighbor.

One way to communicate this in families is to absolve all family members of chores. As disciples of the one who washes feet (see John 13), and the one who calls us to service as the centerpiece of life itself, doing acts of service in the home should not be a "chore"; it is the very essence of life in Christ. According to the standards of the kingdom of God, "Whoever wants to be first must be last of all and servant of all" (Mark 9:35). Here is real life and power. Therefore, absolve one another of any household chores. They are not chores but rather loving acts of kindness. To take out the trash or set the table means that someone else is freed from that activity. These acts of service are ways of saying, "I love you." Paul writes, "So then, whenever we have an opportunity, let us work for the good of all, and especially for those of the family of faith" (Galatians 6:10).

Croaks, Ribbits, and Hops: Service ideas you can try:
   • Do family service in the home (formerly called chores) together . . . no one wants to work alone. Make sure you have a few huddles (pauses for refreshment, food, cheering, storytelling, or games) while doing these loving acts of service. This keeps it fun.

• Adopt a person or family in need. Pray for them every day. Serve them together by doing such activities as mowing their lawn, removing snow, visiting, doing their grocery shopping, bringing them Communion, or making hospital visits. Pool resources and give them a gift on holidays.

• Adopt a person or cause outside your community or country. Work together to provide food for a child in an impoverished land. Be advocates on behalf of the rainforest or some other endangered part of the creation. Help AIDS patients in Africa, earthquake victims, or war refugees. Track their lives through the news, pray for them, and send them needed resources.

• Participate in a mission trip. In one congregation, a group of doctors and nurses go to Jamaica every year and do medical/missionary work. They take their entire families with them.

• Adopt your young adults. Young adults go off to college or the military or a job and find themselves separated from their community. Send them CARE packages, cards, and e-mail. Let them be a part of your family when they are away from home.

• Do dramas and role-playing that re-enact your service. These role-plays can tell the rest of the family or congregation what you have been doing and gets everybody involved in the faith story. Read Deuteronomy 6:20-25. This is a "ah-ha, remember when . . ." account of the Exodus. Use this as a template for your stories that tell of God's "great and awesome signs" (Deuteronomy 6:22).

• Encourage your congregation to develop and promote regular service projects. Because of insurance issues, it is not always easy for families with younger children to have access to some typical public service activities.

• Become advocates for the poor. As a family, join organizations such as Bread for the World and write letters together encouraging the government to help with aid and support for those who cannot help themselves.

• Volunteer at a food shelf, homeless shelter, or jail.

• Become a family tutoring system for children struggling to read. Work with your local school to find out who needs extra help.

NOTES

1. See *Passing on the Faith: A Radical New Model for Youth and Family Ministry* by Merton P. Strommen and Richard A. Hardel (Winona: St. Mary's Press, 2000).

CHAPTER twelve

Frog Habits and Habitats, Key 4—Rituals and traditions

When she goes to bed she has to say goodnight to everyone and everything in a certain order. Her glass of water has to fit into the routine at just the right moment, and when prayers are said, there is a proper order to that, too. Whenever the nighttime formula is disrupted, discontent is voiced. If Daddy forgets to pray for her grandmother or stuffed animals, a scowl crosses her face and accompanying gestures and words are forthcoming. One knows if the nighttime liturgy has been somehow compromised. One knows when she can go to sleep, comforted that the family rites have been properly maintained.

So it is with children. Nighttime rituals are powerfully important. And so it is with teens, young adults, and older adults. We all have need for rituals and traditions to assure us that all is well.

Lily Pad Roots: Routines make us human

Rituals and traditions are those patterns of behavior that occur with regularity. They communicate meaning, values, and relationships that exist between people and with God (including God's created universe). For the Christian community, the way people greet one another each day, the use of a table grace, bedtime prayers, regular congregational worship, the blessing of a Christmas tree, and birthday or baptismal anniversary celebrations are examples of family rituals and traditions that can effectively communicate the good news of Jesus Christ.

Our culture does not support the need for or existence of rituals and traditions, and yet, ample evidence exists demonstrating that human beings continue to use ritual actions to connect the longing for meaning in life with the need for intimate community. We humans remain creatures of habit and ritual whether living in antiquity or postmodernity. Young people especially have been affected by this cultural phenomenon. In one instance, a professor asked a group of college students if young adults believe the use of rituals and traditions is important in their lives. The class responded negatively. The professor then challenged the class by referring them to the pre-game and post-game activities of weekly college football games, including the cheers and dress code of the spectators. The students became aware through this exercise that rituals and traditions are already a part of life.

One student shared that on the previous Easter, her five siblings from ages 15 to 26 were all together for the holidays. The family had a tradition of doing an Easter egg hunt, but this year, supposing the children to be too old, the six Easter baskets were all prepared in advance, filled with Easter eggs already gathered. The student said that she and her siblings mutinied and demanded that the Easter egg hunt never be suspended again.

Tadpole Tale: Rituals help us heal

Ritual acts are not only for worship services, the military, or civic gatherings. Children know the value of repeated actions that bring comfort, meaning, and hope for the future. One missionary family returned home from years of service in New Guinea. Shortly after their return, the father could not handle the transition to the new setting in the United States and ran away from the family, leaving a wife with seven- and five-year-old daughters. It was a traumatic time for the three abandoned family members. The seven-year-old was given the task of setting the dinner table. She continued to set it for four. After about two weeks of this table-setting pattern, her mom put her arms around her daughter and said to her, "Honey, I'm very sorry to tell you, but Daddy isn't coming home anymore. You don't have to set the table for four." The daughter looked up to her mother and responded, "I know, Mommy, I am not setting it for Daddy. I am setting it for Jesus. He will always be here." In the midst of a very troubling and vulnerable time, the little girl needed some assurance that she could see and enact. She found part of it, at least, at the dinner table.

Lily Pad Roots: Rituals root us

Family rituals and traditions serve as a repository that preserves much of a family's history, beliefs, values, hopes, and dreams. Weddings, funerals, and holiday get-togethers provide a few of the memorable and sustaining occasions of family life. All families, indeed all communities, have ritual words, gestures, actions, and traditions that are repeated periodically. The challenge for the church is to help families more consciously and meaningfully participate in these significant rituals and traditions.

The pattern of households gathering for worship on the first day of the week is a New Testament example of ordering life on the basis of the weekly rhythm. Worshiping on Sunday, the first day of the week, reminds Christians of the resurrection of Jesus from the dead. Each Sunday, in fact, is a "little Easter," a moment in time that conveys the hope and faith that is born out of that first Easter, but most Christians in the Western world, one could guess, would find it difficult to explain why Sunday instead of Saturday (the traditional Sabbath) is the day of worship. Here is an instance where the message of the church, embedded in the weekly tradition of Sunday worship, could help individuals and larger households more consciously and meaningfully participate in weekly worship in the congregation. It could also help people recall the value of Sabbath rest and renewal.

The church can take an active role in helping new families identify and claim rituals and traditions that help guide, encourage, and sustain meaningful relationships. Every family engages in patterned behaviors that develop over time in the home. An initial challenge for a new couple establishing their life in their own home is to decide which traditions from their families of origin will be followed. Whose family will be visited for the holidays and when? Are Christmas presents opened on Christmas Eve or Christmas Day? Are birthday celebrations a big deal or something to be acknowledged without too much fanfare? Are hugs, kisses, and verbal affirmations encouraged and how much is enough, too little, or too much?

Tadpole Tale: Rituals help children feel secure

David's son Jeremy set off one morning to catch the school bus. All of a sudden he was in dad's face saying, "You're supposed to say, 'And you, too.'" Jeremy caught dad so off guard that he had to repeat it: "You are supposed to say, 'And you, too.'" Dad tried to capture the meaning of the rather intense, in-your-face directive and realized that Jeremy yelled out to him what they often said to each other when leaving, "Bye, Dad. Love ya. Have a nice day." Dad's response was to have been, "And you, too," but on this particular occasion, Dad was so engrossed with his own activities that he simply mumbled back, "Uh-ha." The parental response was so inadequate that Jeremy turned in his tracks, walked back up the steps and corrected Dad right then and there. Jeremy was in the seventh grade and demanded what all humans demand: proper rituals.

That same evening the whole Anderson family discussed that morning's father-son encounter. They decided to explore ways to greet each other in the morning and say good-bye with words that also conveyed their Christian roots, identity, and hope. It was decided to add a high-five (a common ritual action) along with the words to keep the moments of greeting and departure from appearing too somber or contrived. Over the following months they used a daily greeting when rising, at meals, when leaving one another, or at bedtime. The words were chosen from the language used for each of the church seasons. For Advent they would say to another, "Prepare ye," and the response would be, "The way of the Lord." If it were at the beginning of the day or when leaving, they would often add a high five in the middle of the ritual. For the Christmas season it was "Peace on earth," with the response, "Good will to all." For Epiphany it was "The light of Christ," followed by the high-five and then, "Shines brightly." For Lent it was "Create in me a clean heart, O God," high-five, then, "And renew a right spirit within me." For Easter it was "Christ is risen." "He is risen, indeed," was the response. The high-fives made it fun. Coming at the beginning of rushed work and school days, these greetings brought a breath of fresh, gracious air. At the end of a long, tiring, irritable day, the greetings could bring healing.

Through David's work with congregations, he soon discovered that this activity was transferable to other homes. Greetings in the home for the church year could be taught to children and their parents with delightful as well as humorous results. (For example, one fifth-grade boy added to his Christmas greeting, "To infinity and beyond," a line from the movie Toy Story.) Sharing this little ritual moment for the home worked for pre-schoolers, elementary-aged children, and teens. It worked for aunts and uncles, grandmas and grandpas, as well as brothers, sisters, moms, and dads.

Of course, not all suggestions work equally well for every home or for all time. One year a small rebellion took place in David's own home at Lent. His two teenage children did not want to use the same old greeting as in years past. So, the family went to the Ash Wednesday service without an acceptable Lenten greeting. When they came home from the service Dad said, "I've got it! How about if we use the words from our Ash Wednesday service tonight: 'Remember that you are dust,' and the response would be,

'And to dust you shall return?'" His daughter, Kirsten, said, "In your face." Dad assumed that meant "No."

Somewhat dejected, he went to work the next day and shared his problem with his colleagues. One colleague helped him create a new Lenten response. That day Dad returned home with zeal. When he saw his daughter that evening he said to her, "Kirsten, I have a Lenten greeting for you. Say to me, 'In your face,' and get ready to do a high-five." Kirsten looked at him a little annoyed but sensing it would be easier to amuse Dad than resist, she said, "In your face," and dad responded, "Full of grace." She rolled her eyes and communicated in her own daughter-to-dad style, "No way." In frustration, Dad asked her, "Well, what do you say to your friends at school?" Without hesitation, Kirsten immediately responded, "We say, '*Carpe diem.*'" Dad thought, "What a wonderful Lenten expression: seize the day." So, with Kirsten that Lent, the verbal exchange in the morning and at bedtime and before table graces included *carpe diem*. It worked . . . kind of.

That Lenten season the Anderson family limped along with a combination of "Remember you are dust," "And to dust you shall return," and "*Carpe diem.*" It really was not the most exhilarating Christian exchange that the family had ever come up with, but it endured. It endured with little power or meaning until well into the Lenten season. Late one night, there was a pounding on the door. It was Ann, a neighbor from across the street. She was screaming for help. Mark, her 44-year-old husband and father of two, had just died of a heart attack on the bathroom floor. All were devastated. Both families had been guests in each other's homes. Mark was the outdoorsman who gave Jeremy and David a few pointers on fishing. (To this day, one of Jeremy's prized pictures shows him with a white bass that he had caught from the nearby lake with Dad standing to Jeremy's left, and Mark, the fishing guide for that day, to his right.)

It was an unbelievably sad time. Gloria stayed home that next day to be with Ann and to help plan for the days ahead, including the reception of friends and family. The Anderson family attended Mark's wake and funeral, and joined Mark's family and other friends at the graveside. They hugged one another, committed themselves to be there for Ann and the girls, and they continued their Lenten exchange, "Remember you are dust," "And to dust you shall return." Those words now spoke with a power, intensity, and reality that had not been there before; that God knows about the pain, finality, and grief of death, and God knows—and has not forgotten—Mark. Words that earlier did not seem to speak to modern lives all of a sudden had value. The words became filled with meaning and expressed a longing for something more. The next Easter Sunday, the Andersons went to worship with many others and shouted traditional words that now had new meaning and importance, "Christ is risen; Christ is risen indeed!" During the Easter season the family began and ended their days and included at table grace the words "Christ is risen; Christ is risen indeed! Alleluia!" Mark is not forgotten by God or by the Andersons.

Lily Pad Roots: Rituals span cultures

Simple words can infuse a particular moment with faith, hope, and love, but if the words are forgotten, neglected, left unspoken, or unheard, how can they shape lives? The language of our homes and the gestures and symbols that fill our memories with images of faith and faithfulness only have an impact if used.

Formal greetings between friends, family, and strangers are not new. Every culture has a way of creating a bond between its members through how one says "hello" and "good-bye." The Hebrew word *shalom*, the word for peace and wholeness, is used as a welcoming and departing word and conveys the lasting peace that only God can give between people. A Spanish term for good-bye is *adios,* which literally means, "to God." An expression of departure between Christians in Namibia uses the first portion of the Aaronic benediction, "The Lord bless you and keep you." When Christians in Ghana meet one another, they ask, "How are you?" The response is "By God's grace." Likewise, when asked about the welfare of the family a traditional response is "By God's grace." It is a faithful response that reaches deeply into the soul. When one studies standard greetings for "hello" and "good-bye," one discovers rituals that reveal a deep sense of meaning shaped by a particular faith and values system.

People long for words of grace and blessing. When someone sneezes, one often hears the words "Bless you," or "God bless you." The English word *good-bye* is itself a blessing. The word is formed from a contraction of "God be with ye." In many Latino cultures, when visiting a parent or calling them on the phone, the introductory word is *bendicion,* which means "My blessing, please." Then the parent or older member responds, *"Que Dios te bendiga."* or, "May God bless you." For older generations it would be unheard of to begin a cross-generational encounter without the request for and response of a blessing.

Rituals and traditions are important elements that connect lives and infuse them with a sense of identity, purpose, and meaning. For the Christian community, rituals and traditions speak most effectively when families pay attention to the meaning and value of such actions.

Lily Pad Roots: Rituals, traditions, and Scripture

The Scriptures repeatedly document the human desire for meaningful rituals and traditions. In Joshua 4, after the people of Israel have crossed over the Jordan River on dry ground, God tells Joshua to have a member of each of the 12 tribes take a stone from the Jordan River and place them where the people would camp at night as a memorial shrine. The reason for this ritual is simple. God says, "When your children ask you in time to come, 'What do those stones mean to you?' then you shall tell them that the waters of the Jordan were cut off in front of the ark of the covenant of the LORD . . . So these stones shall be to the Israelites a memorial forever" (Joshua 4:6-7). The ritual action of gathering and depositing the stones became the impetus for cross-generational conversation regarding the faith stories of the adult generations, and a way to pass the faith to future generations.

The gathering of the stones for the sake of teaching children the faith is no isolated formula in the Bible. The Passover festival contains ritual acts that lead the children to ask, "What do you mean by this observance?" (Exodus 12:26). The ritual that leads to the questioning by the children results in storytelling as a teaching tool. The festival of the unleavened bread occurs so that the adults may thereby instruct the young who will then have "the teaching of the LORD" on their lips (Exodus 13:9). The rituals and traditions of Passover "serve for you [the children] as a sign on your hand and as a reminder on your forehead" (Exodus 13:16).

The Gospel of Luke portrays the holy family as people shaped by the rituals and traditions of the Jewish people. Jesus was circumcised on the eighth day and given his name (Luke 2:21). Mary went through the ritual of purification according to the custom. Again, following Jewish custom, Mary, Joseph, and Jesus went to the temple in Jerusalem for the Passover when Jesus was 12 years old. Note that the message of salvation is contained in the ritual signs and acts commanded by God in the Scriptures. The message of salvation continues to shape the lives of children of every age through rituals, traditions, signs, and symbols supported in the life of the home.

Tadpole Tales: Marking your homes

A semi-retired pastor who continues to visit shut-ins noted a change in the interior decoration of the homes he visited. As a young pastor he would often notice a plaque on the wall with a particular saying on it: "Christ is the head of this house, the unseen guest at every meal, and the silent listener of every conversation." Now when this pastor visits homes as a visitation pastor, those signs and symbols are no longer present. Sadly, to this pastor, something of depth was missing; a marking of the Christian faith had disappeared. Through the absence of the plaque, one form of communicating the gospel had fallen silent!

One mother noted the power of signs and symbols on the life of her own daughter. With some level of frustration, the mother observed that when she visited her mother's home with her daughter, the daughter (who was normally rather disruptive), acted quite differently. In Grandma's house, she acted like a "little angel." The mother asked her daughter why it was that she was so well behaved at Grandma's house. The little girl looked at her mother rather incredulously and said, "Well, what else can I do, God is in every room." Mother laughed with delight. As she thought about her mother's home, she could easily visualize the walls of the various rooms. In nearly every room of Grandma's house hung pictures of Jesus or a cross.

Daily life is filled with indicators and messages that shape people's lives. These forms of communication convey meaning, values, faith, and priorities as powerfully as a Sunday sermon. Beginning one's day by reading the newspaper brings a connection to the world around. Similarly, beginning a day with prayer or scripture reading by focusing a religious symbol or message on the wall says, "God is here." Routines, rituals, traditions, signs, and symbols send messages. The question is, *What patterns do families consciously want to use and what messages do they want to send?*

Lily Pad Roots: Rituals and the Christian life

The church has always understood the value of ritual and its impact on the life of the home as well as the practices of the community gathered for worship. The daily office and the hours of prayer shape the day from morning to night. Sunday worship serves as the foundation for the weekly routine. The seasons of the church year are associated with specific colors, stories of the faith, worship services, and ritual activities. All these moments give stability and meaning to the day, the week, and the seasons of the year to remind people of who they are. The rituals and traditions of the church reflect the patterns outlined in the Bible, enabling the people of God to be instructed in the teaching of the Lord.

The medieval church was immersed in such ritual awareness. In the fourteenth and fifteenth centuries, it was not uncommon for a person to recite the Lord's Prayer 30 to 40 times a day. Luther's recommendation to pray the Lord's Prayer morning, noon, and night was actually a simplification of a much more demanding daily pattern.

As a child of the medieval church, Martin Luther had a keen awareness of the power of ritual and tradition. He suggested a tradition for the Christmas season that is popular to this day: the practice of placing an evergreen tree in the home and placing candles on it. The evergreen tree symbolizes the ever-present love of God, and the lights on the tree announce the coming of Jesus, the light of the world that has come into the world. The tree itself recalls that the infant Jesus was born into the world to die for the sins of the world on a tree (see Galatians 3:13-14). The Christmas tree is a pulpit in the home! By its very presence, the tree conveys the message of the good news of Jesus Christ.

Congregations aware of the power of rituals and traditions can assist households to use a variety of means to serve as signs of the Christ story. Throughout the seasons of the church year, the life of the home can announce the good news of Jesus' birth, baptism, teaching, healing ministry, suffering, death, resurrection, and ascension. The Christmas tree and gifts can announce the true intent of the holiday. A house blessing at Epiphany can recount the story of the visit of the Magi and the role of the home as a source of Christian hospitality. Simple disciplines during Lent can help people focus on the magnitude of the gift of God's love and the response of disciples through a life of justice and mercy. Each season has rituals and traditions that can be played out in the home as a means to retell the Christian message. In this way, family rituals and traditions become household pulpits, natural and non-threatening ways to proclaim good news to the world and in the home.

Croaks, Ribbits, and Hops

Many ways exist for households to engage in meaningful remembrances and celebrations. Birthdays, adoptions, baptismal birthdays, dedications, confirmation days, a first driver's license, a first job or a new job, graduations, children leaving home, weddings, anniversaries, divorces, retirements, memorials of various losses, and other moments in the family life cycle are all occasions to celebrate or recall the source of all joy, comfort, and hope. The following are some ideas to engage in rituals in the home:

• Explore with family and friends the traditions and rituals that bind your relationships together. Wonder aloud what those patterns might indicate about your faith and values.

• Create a home altar in your own dwelling space. Consider placing candles, a cross, a Bible, or colored fabric reflecting the church year in that space.

• Look around your own home and identify the faith and values communicated by your interior decorating. Does it say what you want others to know about you? What changes and additions might you make?

• What traditions have you enjoyed from the past that you no longer do? Are some of these traditions that you wish you continued to use in your life? Plan a way to reintroduce one or more of these traditions back into your life.

• Look at the cycle of your days and weeks. When are you productive? When do you enjoy rest and creative play? When do you effectively prepare for either work or recreational time (including rest time)? Does your routine need some adjustments? What can you do to revitalize your routines with constructive work (vocation) time, relaxation time, as well as time to prepare for either? Give attention to your need for sabbath rest. Many of us have lost touch with the biblical idea of sabbath. How can you begin to reclaim some of the refreshment, vitality, and discipleship nurtured by sabbath time? Make a plan to recover some sense of sabbath in your life.

• As you approach the seasons of the year and the seasons of the church year, consider ways to enter them in ways that celebrate the messages, beauty, and hope found in those periods of time.

• Times when you experience a serious loss such as the death of a loved one, a move away from the familiar and secure roots of family and friends, or a family divorce are particular occasions when you need to have the comfort and assurance of your Christian faith. These are also times when faith and assurance can seem far away. During such times, seek the support, comfort, and guidance of your faith by maintaining certain rituals and traditions that have upheld you in the past. Let these human gestures that communicate divine presence be a means to support you through the tough times.

Frogs as AAA Road Servants

Throughout this book we have spoken of the Five Principles for effective faith forma-tion, and we identified Four Key practices. Principles and practices are only as good as the people who understand and live them. Thus, we close by talking about the kind of person needed to make the principles and practices come alive. We call these frogs with legs *AAA Road Servants*. One could say that our model is as easy as 3, 4, 5: AAA Adults, Four Keys, Five Principles.

The kind of person who puts it all together is *authentic, available,* and *affirming* of all people, especially the young. They do this work day in and day out as they seek to live as Jesus' disciples throughout the journey of life. Thus they are road servants.

Tadpole Tale: From taxi driver to spiritual guide[1]

Sitting through our training sessions for more than a day, a baby-boomer mom had the look of love, concern, and stress written on her face. She raised few questions during the training; she was quiet for the most part. Taking things to heart, she pon-dered the words being said about children and youth, and the adults who would raise them. Her presence at the event spoke volumes for the love she had for her own chil-dren, and her discomfort with the direction her parenting was taking. She wanted the best for her children, yet she knew somehow she was missing the boat.

Toward the end of the second day her face lit up. "I've got it," she said. "I'm no longer a taxi driver for my children. I am a spiritual guide to my children." The minivan had taken on a new role: that of chapel. A revolution in self-discovery and self-identity stood before us in the person of this mother.

Lily Pad Roots: The need for a new identity

Within this mother's simple insight and claim of a new personal identity lays the key to the renewal that must sweep through the church frog. Every Christian adult, parent, grandparent, aunt, uncle, friend, godparent, and mentor must come to this realization about himself or herself. Children need more than taxi drivers who transport them to their next soccer game, movie, shopping trip, or school activity. This isn't complete parenting and it certainly isn't Christian parenting. Yet, many of us sense, perhaps grudgingly, that taxi driving is primarily what we do with our children. We transport, haul, drop off, pick up, and otherwise tour our kids through their childhood and early adolescence. Even the church encourages this taxi driver role. We exhort parents to bring their children to Sunday school or church on time so that the spiritual guru's can impart the faith. Leave it to the experts. A bad habit is formed. Whether it is soccer or confirmation, the primary parental task, it seems, is to drive the cab and let the experts impart the skills and the learning.

The family taxi has taken the place of the dinner table in American families. This does not have to be bad news. What the baby-boomer mother discovered is that it is not the act of transporting that is significant, it is what is done on the journey that makes the difference. More significantly, the trip itself is the destination. We are not going somewhere, we *are* somewhere, and what we do in the transporting is significant. Her insight is that renewal begins with herself. In rethinking who she is and her purpose she moves from tour guide, driving her children from event to event, to becoming the event itself and the reason for the trip. She becomes an AAA Road Servant on a Christian pilgrimage with her children!

On the back of many vehicles is an AAA bumper sticker. It guarantees certain services such as towing if the car breaks down, insurance if the driver crashes, and tips if travelers get lost. However, AAA is perhaps best known for its maps and motel services. An AAA "Trip Tick" will show travelers the way to travel safely, and offer suggestions for stopping at interesting points along the way. Also, an AAA hotel guide will provide travelers with hotel information along the journey.

We need AAA in the church. More specifically we need AAA adults who are travelers with children and youth. These adults will "service" our kids when they break down, protect them in a crash, find them when they are lost, and most importantly travel with them using a map that shows the many interesting points and sites of God's world. And we need AAA adults who can show our kids where to rest while on life's journey.

AAA in this sense stands for *authentic, available,* and *affirming.* AAA adults are, first of all, authentic. They walk the talk and are not, in Jesus' words, double-minded (that is, hypocrites; the Greek translation for hypocrites is better stated as double-minded people). An authentic adult engages in daily devotions in his or her own life. They practice the Four Keys. They worship regularly. Their moral and ethical decisions are informed by their faith in Jesus Christ.

Authenticity does not mean perfection, but integrity, character, and the willingness to strive to improve. Authentic people are people who know they need forgiveness and who can forgive others. They are gracious, humble, curious, humorous, and perhaps a bit mischievous. Authentic people know suffering, and they know where to place their trust . . . in Jesus Christ. Authentic adults need not be "cool," or a child's "best friend." If they try to be these things, they are no longer authentic.

Tadpole Tale: Authenticity through suffering

Ralph is authentic. A professor of church history, his life has known great suffering. He has experienced life much like Job in losing three children. He has had personal health problems, and his wife struggles with infection, cancer, and arthritis. By any stretch of the imagination Ralph is not cool. He knows Bach but not the Bare Naked Ladies (the rock band, of course). He reads books about the Reformation of the church, not *Rolling Stone* magazine. Yet, we have witnessed teenagers warm to him as though he were a rock star.

We once asked Ralph to speak to 25 teenagers enrolled in a summer leadership school. We asked him to share his life story, a difficult one that includes the death of his 35-year-old daughter, who left behind a husband and two small children. But in this story, he spoke of Jesus and faith and God's grace in the midst of his pain and suffering. One could hear a pin drop in the chapel that day. Every teenager heard him, identified with him, cried with him, and looked to Jesus with him. Ralph is an AAA Road Servant to these teens. They know his story, they know his heart, they sense his vulnerability and his strength. They know he is of Jesus and so they follow as well.

Lily Pad Roots: Availability

An AAA Road Servant is, secondly, available. Our children and youth have grown up with few adults available to them. We are losing conversation time, play time, reflection time, vacation time, support time, listening time, meal time, and "Four Key time" with our kids. Search Institute recently published new research findings called

Grading Grown-Ups.[2] They found that only one in 20 adults is connected to the lives of young people. In the absence of significant adults, our kids are raising themselves. Their bridge to adulthood rests on the support of peers. Until recently, nearly all human cultures have built a cross-generational bridge to adulthood that includes peers, adults, parents, grandparents, mentors, and larger community structures.

In an informal study, we ask teenagers, "How would you feel if you had a grandparent-type person you could talk to anytime?" Most teens answer in the same way: "Cool!" Then we ask senior citizens, "How would you feel about being available to a teenager who could talk to you when they wanted to?" More often than not we get responses such as, "Oh no, I've done my time," or, "I don't know how to talk to these kids."

We live in the most age-segregated culture in the history of humanity. Our kids want to connect with the adults around them, but they have grown up with adult abandonment. Dr. Roland Martinson reports in his *FaithFactors* research that kids who grew up in the faith report that they could identify at least three adult mentors in their life. These are people who were available to them—not merely parents, but other significant faithful adults as well. To be a person of faith is to be an AAA Road Servant to kids. Adults really don't have a choice. They can only choose to be good at it or not.

Tadpole Tale: Cars for Christ

Jack is an available adult living in a small town in northern Iowa. He is a car nut, a motor head. He loves to work on antique cars. He has a garage and a lot of wrenches (in other words he is ready to do youth ministry!) One Friday evening, Jack received a call from some high school boys from the church. They had a car that needed work and were wondering if they could use Jack's garage. Jack had plans to work on his antique Mercedes over the weekend, but here was a group of guys from his congregation who knew he was available to them. They also knew he had real mechanical skills . . . and a hoist. Jack changed all his plans to spend the better part of the weekend working with these boys. The guys love him; they love working with him. Do you think they'll listen to him when he leads their Sunday school class? Right!

Lily Pad Roots: The need for affirmation

An AAA Road Servant is also affirming. Children and youth need to know that the adults around them are committed to them. The sure and reliable constancy of an adult presence is critical for health and spiritual formation. We need adults who see in youth things they cannot see in themselves.

Tadpole Tale: Big hands and a big heart

Martha and Mel played such a role. They are a retired couple who grew up on farms in the late 1930s. Mel is a carpenter now retired, although it seems he is always fixing something for somebody. People know Martha by her hands. She has big hands . . . huge, in fact. They are hands that have worked hard all their life; that have labored in farm fields from dawn to dusk; that have made countless loaves of bread and cooked innumerable meals; that have held broken people; that have been folded in prayer. They are strong hands, yet when you shake one the squeeze is always gentle; the strength is there not to hurt but to hold. Martha's hands are a reflection of her heart. It is huge as well and works hard, feels deeply, holds gently, and prays earnestly. Martha and Mel are deeply pious and faithful. Jesus is the center for them.

This elderly couple affirmed Allen. Allen was an adolescent who came from an abusive family. No father was in the picture. Rather, Allen lived with his mother, grandmother, and two other siblings. After a long period of abuse by his mother and grandmother, Allen's pastor intervened and he was taken out of his home and placed in an institution for counseling and recovery. The pastor asked Martha and Mel if they could continue their relationship with Allen, a relationship that grew from having taken him to church every Sunday.

For more than two years, while Allen was in treatment, the only adults in his life were Martha and Mel. They visited at least twice every week. They took him home on holidays. Allen seemed to stand taller and walk lighter when he was with them. By contrast, on the rare occasion when Allen's mother would call him, his counselor reported that by the end of the conversation Allen would literally be curled up underneath the desk upon which the phone sat.

Ralph, Jack, the minivan mom, Martha, and Mel all are AAA Road Servants. They are authentic in their faith; they are available to youth, and they are affirming. They are like nuclear energy: they generate heat and light, and they never go away. It is people such as these who make up the legs of the frog. No finer ministers of the gospel exist.

Tadpole Tale: The road to Emmaus and the road to the twenty-first century

The ultimate AAA Road Servant is, of course, Jesus. Two of Jesus' followers were on a road to Emmaus (see Luke 24:13-35). They were discussing the recent events surrounding Jesus' death and resurrection. Like our children, they wandered down the road looking for answers, discussing life's issues, and were probably making decisions without all the information they needed. Jesus interrupted their meandering conversation and gave it focus by interpreting the scriptures for them. Finally, in having a meal with them they see who he really is. Jesus is *authentic,* the Messiah. He is *available* to them on the road at mealtime. And he is *affirming* of them to the point that their hearts burn from within.

Croaks, Ribbits, and Hops

To determine whether you are an AAA Road Servant, or the blessed recipient of another AAA road servant discuss these questions:

- Who was or is an authentic, available, and affirming adult in your life? What did they do? How did you know they cared?
- How do you spend your time? What does this say about your values and priorities?
- How are you available to children and youth? Yours? Others?
- Do you affirm children and youth every day?
- Do you practice the Four Keys with children and youth?
- Identify people in your congregation who are AAA Road Servants. What are they like? What do they do? Are they even aware that they are AAA adults?
- Are you an AAA Road Servant with children and youth? Why or why not? What would have to change in your life in order for you to become one?
- What are the benefits of becoming an AAA traveler?
- Ask children and youth that you know who they think are the AAA Road Servants to them?

Jesus models for us the life he invites us to live. Jesus models for us the church he would have us be: a church with a full body of believers supported on the legs of the church in the home. This church, the church frog with legs, will leap into God's future into the twenty-first century and beyond.

NOTES

1. This story originally appeared in *The Difficult but Indispensable Church,* Norma Cook Everist, ed. (Minneapolis: Augsburg Fortress, 2002), 165-167.
2. *Grading Grown-Ups: American Adults Report on Their Real Relationship with Kids* (Minneapolis: Search Institute, 2001), see www.search-institute.org.